A Treasury of
Critical Thinking Activities
CHALLENGING

Contributors:

Roslind Curtis
Maiya Edwards
Fay Holbert

Editor-in-Chief
Sharon Coan, M.S. Ed.

Art Director
CJae Froshay

Product Manager
Phil Garcia

Imaging
Alfred Lau

Cover Design
Lesley Palmer

Publishers

Rachelle Cracchiolo, M.S. Ed.

Mary Dupuy Smith, M.S. Ed.

Blake Staff

Edited by Kate Robinson

Original cover and internal illustrations by Greg Anderson-Clift

Original internals designed and typeset by Precision Typesetting Services

This edition published by

Teacher Created Materials, Inc.
6421 Industry Way
Westminster, CA 92683
www.teachercreated.com
©2001 Teacher Created Materials, Inc.
Made in U.S.A.
ISBN-0-7439-3619-1

with permission from
Blake Education
Locked Bag 2022
Glebe NSW 2037

Contents

Introduction

Today, teachers face many challenges. One of these is teaching critical thinking skills in the classroom. The teaching and management strategies in this book cater to all students and provide built-in opportunities for bright students. These strategies allow students to actively participate in their own learning. Blackline masters and task cards are ready to use and can easily be added to your existing teaching program.

How This Book Is Structured

Management Strategies

This section describes the key management strategies. Each management strategy is given a symbol which appears on the task cards and blackline masters throughout the book. In this section you'll also find helpful generic blackline masters to support these management strategies.

Teaching Strategies

Seven teaching strategies are targeted:

- Bloom's Taxonomy
- Creative Thinking
- Research Skills
- Questioning and Brainstorming Skills
- Renzulli's Enrichment Triad
- Thinking Caps
- Gardner's Multiple Intelligences

Each of these strategies has its own section with the following parts:

Notes: These provide an overview of the methodology of the teaching strategy and its practical application in the classroom.

Activities: These include a wide range of teaching activities covering the main curriculum areas. They can be undertaken exclusively or in conjunction with activities from the other teaching strategy sections. They could also prompt you to develop your own activities.

Task Cards and Blackline Masters: The activities are supported by a variety of ready-to-use blackline masters and task cards. Suggested management strategies are indicated by symbols in the top right-hand corner.

Management Strategies

by Maiya Edwards

Key Educational Qualities in the Management Strategies for Bright Students

Although the activities in this book are appropriate for all students, they particularly meet the needs of bright students. Linda Silverman, the Director of the Gifted Development Center in Denver, suggests that there are several approaches which work well when dealing with bright students in the classroom.

Find out what they know before you teach them.

This will prevent re-teaching what a student already knows.

Omit drills from their lives.

Bright students often learn and retain a concept the first time it is presented to them. Use drills only for the students who need it.

Pace instruction at the rate of the learner.

As bright students learn quickly, allow them to progress at their own rate.

Use discovery learning techniques.

Inductive learning strategies (such as those explained in the Bloom's Taxonomy model) are welcomed by these students.

Focus on abstract ideas.

Bright students enjoy the challenge of abstract concepts.

Allow them to arrive at answers in their own way.

Bright students enjoy devising their own problem-solving techniques.

Allow students to form their own cooperative learning groups.

Avoid always making the brightest student in the group responsible for the whole group's learning. Allow students to sometimes choose their own groups and work with other bright, motivated students.

Design an individual education plan.

This will cater to different learning rates.

Teach them the art of argument.

Since bright students have a tendency to argue anyway, teach them to understand when it is appropriate to argue and also to understand the reaction of others to their argumentativeness.

Allow students to observe.

Provide bright students with opportunities to observe without demanding immediate answers.

Be flexible in designing programs.

Provide the students with a variety of program alternatives, such as independent study, special classes, mentoring, and enrichment activities.

As many bright students are unable to achieve their full potential in the regular classroom, they can often become frustrated and begin to exhibit disruptive or aggressive behavior. Others withdraw from class activities or deliberately mask their abilities.

Providing activities for the entire class does not mean that the activities need to limit bright students or make them conform. We have devised a range of management strategies for the classroom which allow for the implementation of all the key educational qualities referred to above. Each strategy is practical, flexible, and easy to implement.

As you will see on the next few pages, we have given each strategy an easily recognizable symbol so that when these strategies are applied to the task card and blackline master activities, you will know immediately how to organize your classroom.

Management Strategies for the Mainstream Classroom

A range of classroom management strategies could be employed to promote and encourage the development of the talent of the students in your class. Any of the strategies listed below would help to achieve a positive classroom environment.

Management Strategies Suitable for the Mainstream Classroom

▼   Enrichment and Extension Activities

→   Learning/Interest Centers

●   Contracts

❖   Independent Research

■   Parent Involvement

✖   Peer Tutoring

✳   Competitions and Awards

◗   Mentoring

✶   Team Teaching

✦   Withdrawal Program

⊃   Mixed Ability Grouping

✜   Cluster Grouping

⇒   Vertical Grouping

♣   Field Trips

Below is a sample page from the sections that follow. The symbols relating to the classroom strategies are on the top of each Blackline Master (BLM) or Task Card.

These symbols indicate the best strategies to use.

The learning area utilized for the activity is found here.

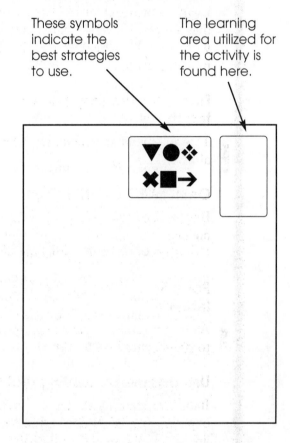

Management Strategies for the Mainstream Classroom

1 ▼ Enrichment and Extension Activities

These can be provided in all subject areas in a variety of ways:

- through task cards or blackline masters for higher level thinking skills
- research tasks
- special "challenge" days
- independent projects
- parent or mentor involvement

See BLM 4

2 → Learning/Interest Centers

These can be established in a corner of the classroom and designed to generate interest in a particular topic. They can

- concentrate on one specific aspect of work being studied, such as weather patterns
- accommodate a special interest such as dinosaurs
- extend certain skills such as advanced language or mathematical skills and thinking skills

See BLMs 4,5,6

3 ● Contracts

Students can be given a range of activities to complete which are set out around the room. Each student is given a list of the activities and asked to mark off each one as it is completed. The flexibility of this contract system appeals to the more capable student.

Contracts also have the advantage of being either teacher initiated or student initiated.

The teacher can set defined, targeted tasks or can allow the students to pursue their own interests with some guidance. There is also flexibility in the time allowed for the contracts. A contract can be extended over many weeks or set as a one night task.

See BLMs 1,2,3,4,7

4 ❖ Independent Research

Independent research provides an opportunity either within the school day or over a longer period to develop personal competencies through individual experiences. It may also involve interaction with others when designated. The research topic can be teacher initiated or student initiated.

It allows the students to launch in-depth investigations into something that they want to find out more about without constant supervision. It also encourages the students to use self-initiative and to employ their own style of learning to produce results.

The teacher's role changes from being the source of all knowledge to that of a facilitator and consultant.

See BLMs 1,2,3,4,7

5 ■ Parent Involvement

Establishing and maintaining a register of parents' interests, abilities, and availability can be invaluable when planning a program for the brighter students in the classroom. Parents can be used to supervise cluster groups or extension activities and to encourage the exploration of individual interest areas. Some of the ways that parents could be kept abreast of classroom activities are via newsletters, resource packs, and information evenings.

Management Strategies for the Mainstream Classroom

6 ✖ Peer Tutoring

The more capable students can be paired with underachievers for some activities. This can be mutually beneficial for both students. The brighter students must develop an ability to clearly communicate an understanding of a topic or problem, while the underachiever receives the benefit of one-to-one coaching.

Outside the mainstream classroom, you can pair more able senior students with bright younger students. For example, pairing grade 6 students with grade 1 students works particularly well. The students could be paired for 30 to 60 minutes per week for activities such as writing, computers, art, or thinking games.

7 ✳ Competitions and Awards

Competition and award schemes such as "Young Innovator of the Year" and "Tournament of the Minds" offer enrichment opportunities for all students but particularly the brighter students. Students within the mainstream classroom could be provided with activities to prepare them for these tournaments and competitions.

Intra-class competitions and awards are a dynamic means of extending the entire class. There is a wide range of options:

- 30-minute quiz challenges.
- knock-out quiz challenges throughout the term or year.
- award schemes for independent research tasks. (bronze award for a written and pictorial presentation; silver if something extra is included, such as a model, video, or Web page; and gold if the project is outstanding.)
- individual point scoring for tasks throughout the year. This scheme works well for all students in the mainstream classroom as points can be awarded for both outstanding work, additional work, or for improvement, effort, and positive attitudes, or for helping others. Points can be exchanged for play money at the end of each term, and students can bid at a class auction for donated items such as books, passes, toys, or for privileges such as extra computer time.

8 ◗ Mentoring

These programs link individual students with community members who have expertise in certain areas. Teachers can establish their own database of suitable people or seek the assistance of their district gifted and talented network to provide them with a list of mentors. Mentors can also talk to the class about specific interest areas and participate in some follow-up activities. This is a very productive way to inspire excellence and encourage independent interests.

9 ✶ Team Teaching

Students with various interests and talents meet with different teachers who specialize in specific subject matters. An excellent way to implement this is for three teachers to nominate three different fields of interest. The students then select which area of interest to pursue. This can be scheduled into the standard teaching week and run for two or three lessons, with a suitable assessment at its conclusion.

10 ◆ Withdrawal Program

Very exceptional students (or "gifted" students) can be withdrawn from a mixed ability class for instruction with other more advanced students. This instruction can be provided by a specially appointed teacher, tutor, or a volunteer.

11 ⊃ Mixed Ability Grouping

When working on class assignments the students are placed in heterogenous groups (that is, groups with a range of abilities). The more able students assume the leadership roles with the others taking the tasks of writing and reporting. Roles can also be interchangeable, or they can be rotated so that an even amount of work is done for all aspects of a task. An ideal size for mixed ability groupings is three to five students.

See BLM 4

12 ✚ Cluster Grouping

All students can be clustered according to their relative ability in the classroom. Higher ability students can occasionally be clustered for full-time instruction within a mixed ability classroom. This works well when compacting a curriculum for the brighter students so that they are able to progress at their own rate.

See BLM 9

13 ⇒ Vertical Grouping

In classrooms which already contain several grade levels, bright students of different ages can be combined with others who have similar interests, abilities, and aptitudes.

See BLM 4

14 ♣ Field Trips

This involves off-campus excursions to meet with experts in various fields, for example: museum experts, marine biologists, and geologists. Field trips can provide an excellent basis for both cluster ability projects or independent research projects.

Self-Evaluation

It should be remembered that self-evaluation is a very powerful form of evaluation and should be an essential component of every classroom evaluation process.

This has been incorporated into the blackline masters on the following pages.

Blackline Masters

A range of blackline masters has been provided which can be used to assess and encourage students when using the above management strategies.

They are not activities in themselves but are designed to support the various teaching strategies presented in the book.

Teacher Records

For your own records and so that you can show parents that you have given their children the opportunity to express the full range of skills, we have provided an individual record sheet suitable for each student, as well as a class record sheet.

See BLMs 7,8

Name: _____

My Research Contract

Research Title: _____

Starting Date: _____ Completion Date: _____

Subject Area: _____

Brief Description: _____

Resources to be used: _____

Method of final presentation: _____

School time allocated to independent research: _____

Home time allocated to independent research: _____

Student's Signature: _____

Teacher's Signature: _____

Self-Evaluation:

The best thing about my independent research was _____

_____

_____

The thing I found hardest to do was _____

_____

_____

I could improve this by _____

_____

_____

Teacher Comment

Name:

My Contract

My contract is to _____

I will start on _____ and finish by _____

✓ When finished	What I will do	How I feel about my work

Teacher Comment

Name:

My Research Checklist

Check (✔) the 3 methods you have used for your independent research and hand in this sheet with your final presentation.

- ☐ Brainstorming
- ☐ Concept Mapping
- ☐ Library Research
- ☐ Interviewing
- ☐ Survey
- ☐ Questionnaire
- ☐ Experiment
- ☐ Graphs/Tables
- ☐ References Cited
- ☐ Have you provided an outline of your project?

Your final method of presentation can be very simple or quite complex. Here are some suggestions. Circle the method you will use.

- Written Report
- Videotape
- Collection
- Letter
- Musical Composition
- Model
- Demonstration
- Scrapbook
- Play/TV Show
- Advertisement
- Comic Strip
- Magazine
- Computer Program
- Panel Discussion
- Invention

- ☐ Final method of presentation chosen
- ☐ Final presentation
- ☐ Own evaluation of the independent study
- ☐ Teacher evaluation of the independent study

Self-Evaluation

Name:

Checklist for Group Work

Other Group Members: _____

☐ I contributed new ideas. The best idea was _____

☐ I listened to the ideas of others. The best idea was _____

☐ I encouraged others in my group. This was by _____

☐ Something I could improve on is _____

_____

_____

Name:

Questionnaire for Learning Center or Enrichment Activities

Task: _____ Time taken: _____

How I did the activity and what I thought of it: _____

_____

_____

Future activities I would like included: _____

_____

_____

Name:

Learning Center Evaluation Sheet

ACTIVITY	DATE COMPLETED	EVALUATION (for example: too hard, too easy, boring, interesting)

Teacher Comment

Name:

Concept Mapping

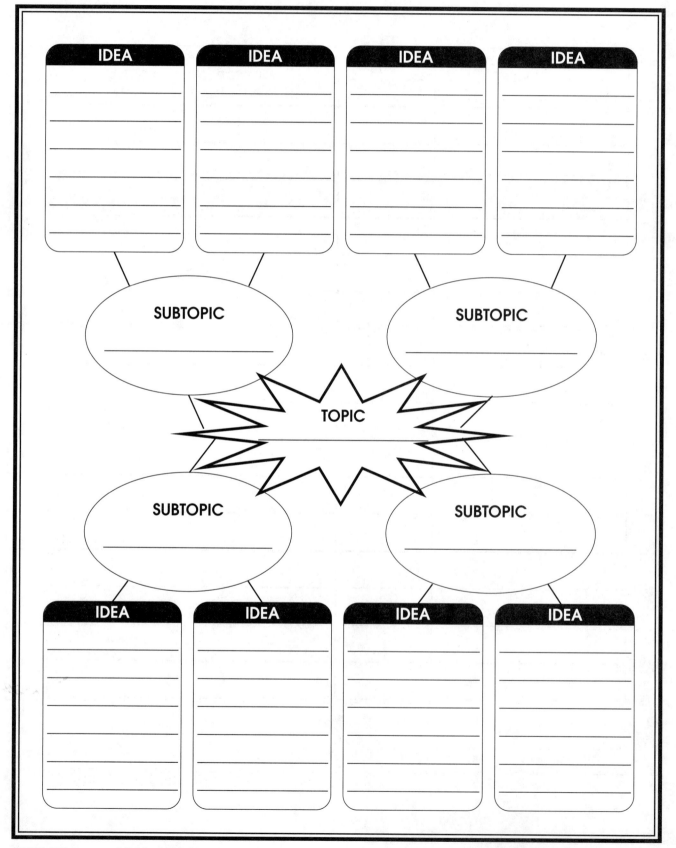

Individual Record Sheet

Extension Procedures

Student Name: _____ Grade: _____

Students should complete at least one task or BLM from each extension procedure.

EXTENSION PROCEDURE	CARDS/BLMs COMPLETED (Circle when finished)							
Bloom's Taxonomy (BT)	1	2	3	4	5	6	7	8
Creative Thinking (CT)	1	2	3	4	5	6	7	8
Research Skills (RS)	1	2	3	4	5	6	7	8
Questioning/Brainstorming (QB)	1	2	3	4	5	6	7	8
Renzulli's Enrichment Triad (RT)	1	2	3	4	5	6	7	8
Thinking Caps (TC)	1	2	3	4	5	6	7	8
Gardner's Multiple Intelligences (GI)	1	2	3	4	5	6	7	8

Teacher Comment

Class Record Sheet

Extension Procedures

Check that each student has completed at least one card
or BLM from each extension procedure.

STUDENT NAME	BT	CT	RS	QB	RT	TC	GI	COMMENT

Register of Parents' Interests

PARENT'S NAME	CHILD	CONTACT DETAILS	AVAILABILITY	AREA/S OF INTEREST

Bloom's Taxonomy
Notes and Activities

by Maiya Edwards

Overview for the Classroom Teacher

Bloom's Taxonomy

This model is one of the most frequently used extension procedures, for the development of higher level thinking skills. These skills are applicable to any subject and to any level of education, from pre-school to tertiary. Many varied teaching and learning activities can be developed using this as the basis.

The model enables all students to work through the process of developing a concept, with the more advanced students spending longer at the higher levels than the average student.

The thought processes involved in the different levels:

1. KNOWLEDGE — to recognize, list, name, read, absorb
2. COMPREHENSION — re-state, describe, identify, review, explain
3. APPLICATION — apply, illustrate, connect, develop, use
4. ANALYSIS — interpret, categorize, contrast, compare, classify
5. SYNTHESIS — plan, create, invent, modify, revise
6. EVALUATION — judge, recommend, assess, criticize, justify

Average Student

1. Knowing and recalling specific facts

2. Understanding the meaning from given information

3. Using previously learned information in new situations

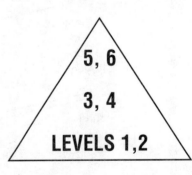

Talented Student

4. Breaking up the whole into parts

5. Putting together the parts to form a new whole

6. Making value judgements

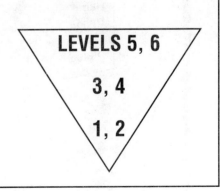

Overview for the Classroom Teacher

From Convergent to Divergent Thinking

Use the actions . . . . to achieve these outcomes.

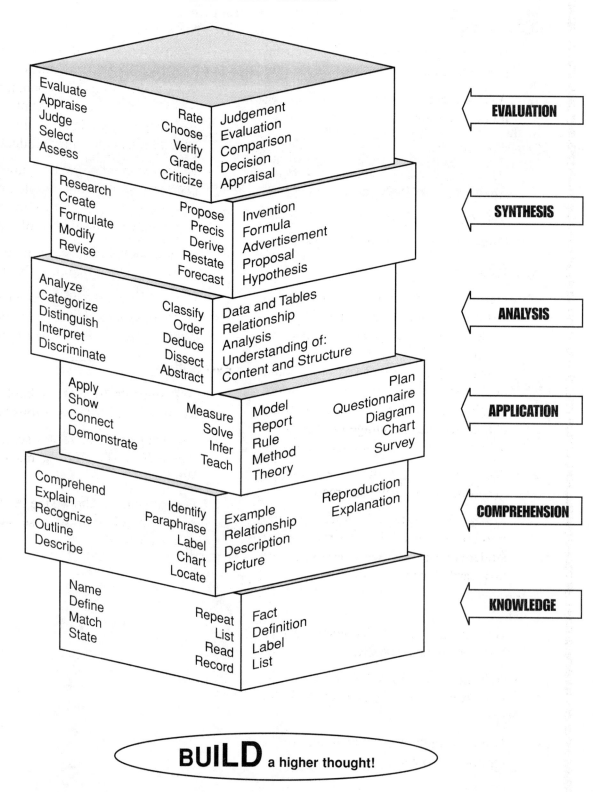

Evaluate	Rate	Judgement
Appraise	Choose	Evaluation
Judge	Verify	Comparison
Select	Grade	Decision
Assess	Criticize	Appraisal

EVALUATION

Research	Propose	Invention
Create	Precis	Formula
Formulate	Derive	Advertisement
Modify	Restate	Proposal
Revise	Forecast	Hypothesis

SYNTHESIS

Analyze	Classify	Data and Tables
Categorize	Order	Relationship
Distinguish	Deduce	Analysis
Interpret	Dissect	Understanding of:
Discriminate	Abstract	Content and Structure

ANALYSIS

Apply	Measure	Model	Plan
Show	Solve	Report	Questionnaire
Connect	Infer	Rule	Diagram
Demonstrate	Teach	Method	Chart
		Theory	Survey

APPLICATION

Comprehend	Identify	Example	Reproduction
Explain	Paraphrase	Relationship	Explanation
Recognize	Label	Description	
Outline	Chart	Picture	
Describe	Locate		

COMPREHENSION

Name	Repeat	Fact
Define	List	Definition
Match	Read	Label
State	Record	List

KNOWLEDGE

BUILD a higher thought!

Bloom's Taxonomy for English

Theme: Humor in Writing

Knowledge

- Have students brainstorm the sort of things that make them laugh.

- Ask students to name some of the humorous books they have read.

Comprehension

- Have students retell some of the funny stories they have read.

- Ask them to describe some of the humorous characters in the books.

Application

- Cut out some cartoon characters and paste them on a sheet of paper. Have students work in groups to list the characteristics of each character. For example, Lucy from "Peanuts" could be described as bossy, loud, opinionated. Give each group three characters and encourage them to write a comprehensive list of characteristics.

- Ask students to write a report on a humorous book they have read.

- Study the style of limericks and humorous poems in general. Have students write their own versions. (see task cards for ideas)

Analysis

- Ask students to identify what makes a book or character funny.

- Ask them to think of some of the humorous things the characters did or said.

- Write a biography of an author of humorous books.

Synthesis

- Brainstorm a list of crazy or off-beat things to sell. Examples could be birthday parties on the moon, ice cream pizzas, or back-to-front shoes. Challenge students to write advertisements for their product.

- Have students make up funny characters to do the sales pitch for their advertisements. Ask them to role-play their character for the rest of the class.

- Have students make up a funny jingle about something that they like to eat.

- Cut out a variety of different cartoon characters and challenge students to create new cartoons of their own.

Evaluation

- Ask students to write a book review about their favorite humorous book.

- Ask students if there are some things they believe shouldn't be made fun of. Why?

- Form a panel to choose the ten funniest poems or jokes from those submitted by the class.

BLOOM'S TAXONOMY

English

BLM 10

Name:

Management Strategies:

▼ → ● ❖

Future of the World

Comprehension

Write a brief outline of some of the changes that have taken place in your lifetime.

_____

_____

_____

_____

_____

_____

_____

_____

_____

_____

_____

_____

_____

_____

_____

_____

Knowledge

Make a time line of important events in the history of the world.

Year   Event

Year	Event
_____	_____
_____	_____
_____	_____
_____	_____
_____	_____
_____	_____
_____	_____
_____	_____
_____	_____
_____	_____
_____	_____
_____	_____
_____	_____
_____	_____
_____	_____
_____	_____
_____	_____
_____	_____
_____	_____
_____	_____
_____	_____
_____	_____
_____	_____

Application

Illustrate one

of the changes

in a cartoon strip.

Name: _____

Future of the World

Analysis

Design a questionnaire to collect data about what people expect of the future. Analyze and present your findings.

_____
_____
_____
_____
_____
_____

Evaluation

Select 3 major problems facing the world today.

1. _____

2. _____

3. _____

What are your solutions?

_____
_____
_____
_____
_____
_____
_____
_____
_____
_____
_____
_____
_____
_____
_____
_____
_____
_____
_____

Synthesis

Design a school of the future that would really appeal to children. Sketch and label some of your ideas below.

Magic and Make-Believe

What if Cinderella's fairy godmother could perform some magic for the three little pigs and the big bad wolf? What do you think they would ask for?

Computer Complaints

If computers could talk, what do you think would be the ten major complaints they would have?

Alice in the Future

Re-title the story *Alice in Wonderland* and set it in the year 2050.

My Invention

What funny invention could this be?

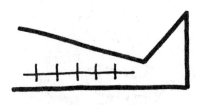

Bloom's Taxonomy for English

Application, Analysis, Synthesis, Evaluation

Come to My Party!

Make up a party list of your five

favorite humorous characters.

Design some party games

they may like to play.

A Modern Nursery Rhyme

Here is one version of a

traditional nursery rhyme

placed in a modern-day setting:

Little Jack Horner

Sat in a corner

Working on his PC

As he checked his-email

He let out a wail

"No one is writing to me!"

Choose your own nursery rhyme

and adapt it to the present day.

What a Stink!

The answer is "stinky socks"!

Write five questions.

A Funny Speech

Your favorite funny character

has been asked to give

a talk at your school.

Write his/her speech.

Bloom's Taxonomy for Math

Knowledge

- Explain and demonstrate mathematical concepts using practical and real-life situations, for example, students using one color then adding two others, or two students sharing six pencils.

- Encourage discussion among pupils and between pupils and the teacher. Students who grasp concepts more quickly should be encouraged to help the slower students.

- Ensure students have regular practice in fundamental number skills. A certain time should be set aside each day for this.

- Have students develop automatic recall of number facts. Use a combination of tables, games and everyday problems, for example 2 x 2 = 4 tables could be reinforced by using an everyday problem such as: "Tim and Sara each have two blocks. How many do they have altogether?"

Comprehension

- Working in pairs, have students take turns demonstrating number facts to each other, using concrete representation. For example: 163 x 2 could be demonstrated with MAB blocks.

Application

- Encourage students to transfer their skills to other subject areas, for example they could apply measuring, estimating, and the use of shapes when making models or charts. This would transfer their mathematical skills to other subjects such as science, social studies, or art.

- Have students work in groups to list all the situations in their homes where they

would use calculations. Examples would be counting money, estimating time, adding up bills.

- Ask all students to think of a question for which the answer could be written as a graph, for example: "How many days has it rained this week?"

Analysis

- Stimulate students to think about their number problems with questions like these: What would happen if you left out a zero? Where might this measurement be used in real life? How did you arrive at that answer?

- Have students use the telephone directory to find numbers which add up to 30.

- Have students work in pairs to explain fractions to their partner using pieces of paper. They could start with simple fractions such as one-half or one-quarter and proceed to more complex fractions.

Synthesis

- Ask students to think of ten uses for a meter of string.

- Have students work in groups to design a quiz show based on numbers.

- Draw a picture using only straight lines.

Evaluation

- Brainstorm all the reasons that estimating is an essential skill to have.

- Have students recommend some changes to the present math curriculum based on things they have studied earlier in the year.

Bloom's Taxonomy for Math

Analysis, Synthesis, Evaluation

Number System

Invent a new number system.

Write and solve five problems using the new symbols.

Handshakes

There are eight people at a party. If a person shakes hands with everyone at the party, how many handshakes will there be?

Extension:
How many handshakes would there be
in your family?
in your class?
if all the boys shook hands with the girls?

Time Table

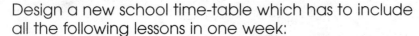

Design a new school time-table which has to include all the following lessons in one week:

English (7 hours)   Social Studies

Math (5 hours)   Spanish

Health & PE (2 hours)   Music

Science and Technology   Art

Handwriting   Free Choice

Bloom's Taxonomy for Math

Analysis and Synthesis

Population

Find out what the population of the United States was in: 1800
1850
1900
1950
1999

Chart these figures on a graph.

Estimate what the population will be in 2050.

World Time

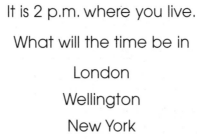

It is 2 p.m. where you live.

What will the time be in

London

Wellington

New York

Tokyo?

Lilies

Water lilies double in area every 24 hours.

At the beginning of summer there is one water lily on the lake.

It takes 60 days for the lake to be completely covered.

On what day is it half covered?

Magic and Make-believe

Here are some problems for you to research.

They all require a prediction and then the right answer.

1. How much money is there in three yards of ten-cent pieces?

    My prediction is _____

    The answer is _____

2. How many words are on the front page of today's newspaper?

    My prediction is _____

    The answer is _____

3. How many bricks are on the outside structure of the school building?

    My prediction is _____

    I calculated the right answer by _____

    _____

    The answer is _____

4. How high is the school flagpole?

    My prediction is _____

    I calculated the right answer by _____

    _____

    The answer is _____

5. How much space is needed to store a collection of 300 video cassettes?

    My prediction is _____

    I calculated the right answer by _____

    _____

    The answer is _____

Name: _____

Management Strategies:

Number Trivia

How many number questions can you answer?

1. Who is code-named Agent **007**? _____

2. How many dog years are there for every human year? _____

3. How many years are there in one decade?   _____

    one score?   _____

    one century?   _____

    one millennium? _____

4. How many cards are in a full deck, excluding jokers? _____

5. What is the **747**? _____

6. Who wrote these books?

    20,000 *Leagues Under the Sea?*   _____

    Around the World in **80** *Days?*   _____

    101 *Dalmatians?*   _____

    1984   _____

7. Think of 3 questions of your own.

    Write them on the back of this page or on a seperate sheet of paper.

Theme: Pollution

Knowledge

- Challenge the class to define what pollution is.

- List the different types of pollution such as air, noise, water.

- Read about the causes and effects of pollution. Have students list them under "Cause" (for example, car exhaust fumes) and "Effect" (for example, smog).

- Brainstorm things that are being done to combat the effects of pollution: in the United States, in your state, in your local area.

Comprehension

- Ask students to provide a definition of pollution.

- Ask students to select one type of pollution and describe it in detail.

- Have students create a collage of the effects of pollution.

Application

- Encourage students to give examples of pollution from their own experiences. Ask them questions like, "What example of pollution are you aware of in your local community?" "Why is it a problem?" "How long has it been a problem?" "What attempts have been made to clean up the pollution?" "How successful have the remedial efforts been?"

- Have students choose one type of pollution in their local area and depict its effects by means of photographs, an illustration, or a model.

Analysis

- Have students analyze the main problems caused by the pollution they have discussed. Ask them to present a list of possible solutions to attach to their model or illustration.

- Ask students to examine their household trash and then construct a graph to show the different categories.

Synthesis

- Have students predict how the United States could change as a result of increased air and water pollution.

- Have students work in groups of 4 or 5 to produce a short play about one major problem caused by pollution.

Evaluation

- Ask students to choose one example of pollution in their local area that they consider to be a serious problem. Have them write a letter to the state government, outlining their concerns and providing possible solutions.

Name:

City of the Future

TASK 1: Design a model of a city of the future which will have no pollution problems.

TASK 2: Explain how you would solve potential pollution problems in your city.

My **city of the future** would be called _____

POTENTIAL PROBLEM	SOLUTION
Household trash	
Polluted drinking water	
Air pollution from cars	
Air pollution from factories	
Noise pollution from cars and planes	

Teacher Comment

Name:

Pollution

Management
Strategies:

Evaluation

BLOOM'S
TAXONOMY

Science

BLM 15

1. Pollution is a necessary part of modern life.   Agree / Disagree

    Justification:

    _____

    _____

2. Household waste can easily be reduced.   Agree / Disagree

    Justification:

    _____

    _____

3. Pollution is not a problem in our local environment.   Agree / Disagree

    Justification:

    _____

    _____

4. The media exaggerates pollution problems.   Agree / Disagree

    Justification:

    _____

    _____

5. All countries should use nuclear power   Agree / Disagree

    because it produces cheap electricity.

    Justification:

    _____

    _____

Teacher Comment

Bloom's Taxonomy for Creative Arts

Theme: Music

Knowledge

- Ask students about the music they like to listen to. Discuss the different types ranging from traditional to contemporary styles.
- Have students list musical instruments. Ask them to describe the types of sounds they make.

Comprehension

- Ask students to give examples of contemporary music.
- Play some contemporary and some classical music to the class. Ask students to locate which instruments are being used in different pieces of music.

Application

- Find or make an instrument which can create a sound you might hear in traditional music. Write these sounds down and play them.
- Survey the class to find out their favorite kinds of music.

Analysis

- Search the school library for compact disks or audiotapes of music from several cultures. You can also visit music Internet sites such as *www.goodnoise.com*. Compare these music types. Ask students to record similarities and differences as you play the music.
- Play a traditional piece of music and ask students to interpret its meaning.
- Have students record various sounds of nature (such as rain, wind, or rustling leaves) and ask them to decide which would be suitable as the background for a piece of music.

Synthesis

- Ask students to investigate how they can use things around them to produce music, for example, bird calls or blowing across glass bottles.
- Find a story that could be set to music. Talk about what sort of music would suit each character. Create rhythms to represent the changing moods of different parts of the story.
- Have students plan Music Day. Contact a local cultural organization to advise you on indigenous music and culture. Have them come in and talk to students and assist in the planning. Aim for a balance of contemporary and traditional music.

Evaluation

- Have students rank singers or bands from their most to least favorite. Ask them to justify their rankings.
- Evaluate the success of your Music Day and decide what you could do to improve it.

Name:

Story Music

TASK 1: Choose a story that lends itself to music.

TASK 2: Write a song about one of the characters in the story.

_____

_____

_____

_____

_____

_____

TASK 3: Write a song about one of the places in the story.

_____

_____

_____

_____

_____

_____

TASK 4: List the musical instruments you will use to accompany your songs.

_____

_____

_____

_____

_____

Teacher Comment

Bloom's Taxonomy for Creative Arts

Application, Analysis, Synthesis, Evaluation

Musical Instrument

What sort of traditional musical instrument could you make out of this?

Planning an Escape

If you were stranded on a desert island with only a didgeridoo, clapping sticks, and a boomerang, how would you use these to help you escape?

Yothu Yindi

The answer is Yothu Yindi.

Make up six questions.

Alphabet Music

For each letter of the alphabet name something that could be used to make traditional or contemporary music.

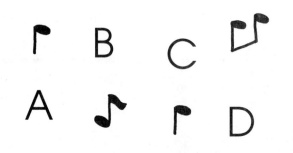

Make Your Own Task Cards

Creative Thinking
Notes and Activities

by Maiya Edwards

Overview for the Classroom Teacher

Creative Thinking Skills

In this section we are trying to move away from verbal and deductive skills and convergent thinking at factual levels to encourage originality, inductive and inferential skills, and divergent thinking.

By recognizing and encouraging the potential of creative thinking in the classroom, the teacher can equip students with the open-ended, divergent thinking skills that are so useful in an ever-changing world.

Creativity can be developed in all students. This can be done by encouraging students to become independent thinkers who can modify, adapt to, and improve the classroom environment. Teachers should encourage adventure and speculation by creating a positive atmosphere in which there is freedom to reflect, experiment, and take risks.

We can look at the creative process in five stages. Each of these stages involves the thinking skills and feelings which make up creativity.

Problem Awareness

This stage requires the ability to recognize that a problem exists, as well as **sensitivity** and **awareness**.

Problem Definition

The second stage involves stating a problem in a meaningful way so that it is easily understood and therefore requires **imagination, curiosity,** and **originality**.

Incubation of Ideas

The third stage involves the production of intuitive and original possible answers, before the facts have been checked out. Therefore, this synthesizing process of blending the old with the new requires **fluency, flexibility, originality, elaboration, risk-taking,** and **imagination.**

Illumination

The fourth stage requires the **awareness** necessary to provide an instant insight into the solution, often referred to as the 'Aha!' moment.

Evaluation

The final stage requires the **perseverance** to evaluate the validity and full impact of the ideas generated.

Encouragement of creativity requires activities to challenge both thinking skills and emotional responses. This can be done by providing a supportive and stimulating classroom environment which will nurture these processes. On the following page are some ways in which the creative elements of thinking and emotional response can be enhanced.

Overview for the Classroom Teacher

Creativity Catalysts

Creativity catalysts can be used to generate innovative and original ideas.

Fluency

This initial stage combines the thinking skill of fluency with the emotional responses of imagination, curiosity, and originality to generate many different ideas, possibilities, and solutions.

Creativity catalysts

- How many ways ...?
- List all the possible uses… .
- Think of all the problems… .
- Give as many ideas as you can… .
- Add to this list… .

Flexibility

This stage combines the thinking skill of flexibility with the emotional response of sensitivity to allow the students to blend the old with the new, and to see things from many different points of view.

Creativity catalysts

- What is the relationship between…?
- If you were…?
- Categorize… .
- Rearrange… .
- Substitute... .

Originality

This stage combines the thinking skill of originality with the emotional responses of risk-taking and imagination. It encourages students to be inventive and use unique and unexpected approaches.

Creativity catalysts

- Create… .
- Design a different way to… .
- How would you…?
- Invent… .
- Predict…

Elaboration

This final stage combines the thinking skill of elaboration with the emotional responses of awareness and perseverance. It encourages students to expand, develop, and add to ideas and materials.

Creativity Catalysts

- Add details to… .
- Plan… .
- Expand… .
- Combine… .
- Decide… .

For more useful classroom catalysts, use the mnemonic **CREATIVITY** to generate further extension activities.

C Combine, integrate, merge, fuse, brew, synthesize, amalgamate

R Reverse, transpose, invert, transfer, exchange, return, contradict

E Enlarge, magnify, expand, multiply, exaggerate, spread, repeat

A Adapt, suit, conform, modify, alter, emulate, copy, reconcile

T Thin out, minimize, streamline, shrink, squeeze, eliminate, understate

I Instead of, substitute, swap, replace, exchange, alternate, supplant

V Viewpoint change, other eyes, other directions, more optimistically, more pessimistically

I In other sequence, rotate, rearrange, by-pass, vary, submerge, reschedule

T To other uses, change, modify, re-work, other values and locations

Y Yes! affirm, agree, endorse, concur, approve, consent, ratify, corroborate

Creative Thinking for English

Theme: Poetry

Many students have a love of words and are captivated by the rhythm and imagery in language. Poetry is a flexible and creative medium through which students are given the opportunity to use their imaginations and express their ideas.

The teacher can provide all students with the opportunity to study the structure and forms of poetry, which will extend their creative thinking skills. This can be done by ensuring that the four elements of creative thought are encouraged in the classroom.

Fluency

- Have students list their favorite poems.
- Ask students to list different themes for poetry. Examples are nature, animals, and people.
- Brainstorm words that could be used for each different theme.
- Ask students how many different styles of poems they can think of, for example, haikus, limericks, rhyming couplets, and free verse.
- Have students provide examples of the different styles.
- Ask students which poems make them laugh or make them sad.
- Have students give examples of similes and metaphors.

Flexibility

- Categorize poems under the headings of: rhyming, free verse, nonsense poems, and so on.
- Ask students to think of different ways to group poems. For instance, under author, theme, or shape.
- Have students list the ways in which free verse and rhyming poems are different. Then list the ways they are the same.
- Ask students to nominate their favorite poets and give reasons for their choices.
- Have students finish similes such as: "It's as warm as…" or "I'm as happy as …"

Originality

- Challenge the students to create a new form or style of poetry.
- Have students write a poem about how sunshine would sound.
- Have students work in groups to create a poem that combines words and sounds, for example, a poem about a kettle boiling or someone playing a computer game.
- Ask students to imagine that they have interviewed a favorite singer. Have them write the whole interview (questions and answers) in verse.
- Have students find poems that describe the elements of nature. Ask them to analyze the types of words and images that are used and then write their own.

Elaboration

- Have students change "Twinkle Twinkle Little Star" into a rhyme about a wishing star.
- Ask students to write a poem that combines the attributes of a cat, a football, and popcorn.
- Have students use their names to write an acrostic poem.
- Have students rewrite a well-known nursery rhyme or poem with the addition of a new character, for example, Old Mother Hubbard's pet lizard.
- Have students change a happy poem or nursery rhyme into a sad one or vice versa, for example, "Old King Cole was a sad old soul…."
- Write a round shape poem and then add new words to it to make it into the shape of a heart.
- Write a class poem starting with a funny line like: "Yuk! Bubblegum in my hair!" Pass it on to the next person, and so on, until every person has written one line.
- Make a "poet-tree" in your classroom. Have students display information about their favorite poets, poems, similes, and metaphors.

Creative Thinking for English

A Chewy Discovery

In 1872 an American photographer was trying to develop a substitute for rubber from the gum of a chicle tree. While working he put some of the gum in his mouth and started to chew.

That was how chewing gum was discovered.

Write a poem describing this discovery.

Weather Forecast

Imagine you are a weather forecaster. Write out the weather forecast in the form of a shape poem for:

- a sunny day

- a wet day

- a tornado

Theme Poems

Pick a theme that you like, such as sports, animals, or feelings. Collect poems that relate to that theme.
Put them in a book or folder and make up a poem of your own on the same theme.

Emotion

Choose an emotion like anger, happiness, or fear. Write a poem about it using this formula:
- What color is the emotion?
- What does it taste like?
- What does it smell like?
- What does it look like?
- What does it sound like?
- What does it feel like?

Creative Thinking for English

▼ ● ■

Constitution

Obtain a copy of the preamble to the Constitution.

Using free verse or rhyme, write your own preamble for the Constitution.

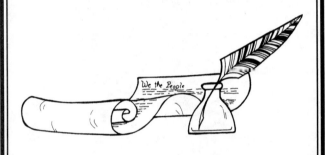

▼ ● ■

Poetry

Bring in photographs of things that interest you. Then write poetry that describes actions, impressions, feelings, or places represented in the photos.

▼ ● ■

Someone You Admire

Choose a person you greatly admire.

Make a list of adjectives, similes, and metaphors to describe this person.

Use these to write a poem dedicated to him/her.

▼ ● ■

Nonsense Poem

Write a nonsense poem that has the following in every line:

- a body part and a famous person
- a kitchen utensil and a dance
- a color and a noise

Creative Thinking for English

An Everyday Object

Find three examples of poems written about everyday objects.

Write your own poem about a common object in your home or your classroom, for example,

- an ode to a paper bag
- a limerick about a can of baked beans
- a rhyme about a pair of sneakers

Obituary

Select a poet whose poems you like. Explain why the poetry appeals to you.

Present this information in the form of an obituary. Check the newspaper for examples of different types of obituaries.

Group Poem

Work in a group of four. Each person should select at least two favorite lines of poetry and read them to the rest of the group.

Create your own group poem by using words or even whole lines from these poems.

Give your poem a title and put it up on the wall for others to read.

Epitaph

Research how an epitaph is written.

Write an epitaph about a real or imaginary pet.

Creative Thinking for English

New Age Poem

Write a poem depicting life in the year 2500.

Present it in an innovative way with a new language, new form, or new structure.

Poetry from Different Cultures

Research poems from two different cultures. You could choose from bush ballads, Aboriginal poetry, rap, hip hop, reggae, African chants, etc.

Compare and contrast the two forms and give reasons for the type you prefer.

Write a poem of your own modeled on one of the cultures you have chosen.

Ice Cream Poem

Imagine you have been asked to write a poem about ice cream.

Think about…

…the **form**. Will it be a limerick, nursery rhyme, chant, or free verse?

…the **structure**. Will it contain similes and metaphors?

…the **visual impact**. Will it be a shape poem or a haiku?

Outer Space Poem

The television series "Star Trek" begins with these words:

"Space, the final frontier. These are the voyages of the Starship Enterprise; its continuing mission to explore strange new worlds; to seek out new life and new civilizations; to boldly go where no one has gone before."

Write your own preamble to a new television series set in outer space.

Creative Thinking for Math

Encourage creative thinking in math by beginning each lesson with a quick challenge to students related to the unit of work they are about to study. This will focus the students' thinking and encourage active participation in the lesson right from the start. It will also help to create a more positive attitude towards the learning process.

Fluency

Encourage students to think about the thinking skills and inquiry processes required for solving problems. Encourage them to brainstorm ideas and come up with a lot of solutions and possibilities. Stimulate discussion with questions like these:

- What animals can run faster than man?
- The answer is 100. What are ten questions?
- List all the things in the classroom that are shaped like cylinders.
- How many different ways of measuring time can you think of?

Flexibility

Expand brainstorming activities by adapting and extending them. Suggestions:

- Group the cylinder shapes according to size and weight.
- How many other ways can you group these objects?
- What reasons can you give for changing the way we measure time?
- How many uses can you find for a yard of string?
- Find five different objects that are the same size, weight, or shape. List all the ways they are different.
- What are the similarities between a lunchbox and a mailbox? Think in terms of sizes, colors, uses, materials, parts and shapes.

- If you have four coins, how much money could you have?

Originality

Encourage originality by asking open-ended questions, providing students with more opportunities to think in the abstract, and rewarding creative and innovative solutions. Suggest to the students the following:

- Design a math puzzle for the teacher and others in the class to solve.
- Write a story about 5 x 4 = 20 based on your family.
- Find a different way to measure a year. Create a new calendar.
- Invent a new way of measuring space and weight.
- Everyone you see is walking around backwards. Give three mathematical reasons for this.

Elaboration

Have students work in groups or individually to reflect upon the previous three processes. Ask them to look at alternatives, expand on ideas, and add more details with activities such as those suggested below:

- Make this shape into a different more, complicated form: ø
- Build a scale model to represent your classroom.
- Change a pyramid shape to something different by using BAR. (Make it **b**igger, **a**dd something, and **r**eplace something.) Draw your new shape.
- Draw a maze in the first initial of your name.
- Calculate the best area in the school playground where a new swimming pool could be placed. Draw your plan to scale. For example, 1 inch = 1 yard
- Imagine that you have just won $1,000. Itemize how you would spend it.

Name:

Management
Strategies:

▼ →

CREATIVE
THINKING

Math

BLM 17

A Model of a Pyramid

You will need these items:

scissors, cardboard, copy of a triangle shape to trace around, ruler, tape,
glue

Directions

1. Trace the shape of the triangle onto four pieces of cardboard.

2. Cut out all four triangles.

3. Lay the four triangles on your desk with the long edges together and
    tape the seams.

4. Draw a perfect square with sides of 20 cms on your cardboard.

5. Cut out the square.

6. Fold the triangles to a pyramid shape and stand them on the square.

7. Tape them securely.

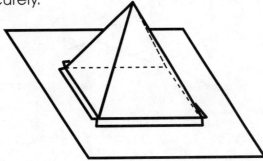

Extension

Choose a shape like a cube or a cylinder, or something even more
challenging, and write out instructions for how to make this shape. Think
carefully about each instruction. When you have finished, give your
instructions to a friend to follow.

Name:

Rectangle Mobile

Step 1: On a piece of cardboard, draw three rectangles measuring 8 inches (21 cm) x 5 inches (13 cm).

Step 2: Mark two of the rectangles "A" and the third one "B."

Step 3: Cut out the rectangles.

Step 4: On both rectangles A, measure 1½ inches (3.5 cm) from the top then draw a dotted line down the center measuring 5 inches (14 cm) as shown below.

Step 5: On rectangle B, measure 3 inches (4 cm) from the top and then draw a dotted line down the center to the bottom measuring 5 inches (17 cm) as shown below.

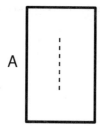

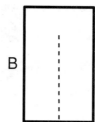

Step 6: Cut along the dotted lines.

Step 7: Join rectangles A and B together as shown in the diagram below.

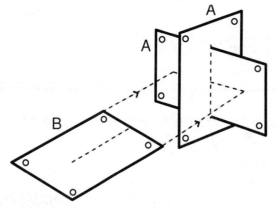

Step 8: With a paper punch make a hole in each corner of each rectangle.

Step 9: Thread colored yarn through the holes to form triangles.

How many triangles can you form? _____

If you have laced 20 triangles, what is the name of your shape?

Creative Thinking for Math

Cryptic Numbers ▼ → ★

Test your skills on these cryptic numbers:

Example: 12: M in a Y   Answer: 12 months in a year

1. 2: E in a H
2. 4: S in a Y
3. 12: D of C
4. 4: L on a D

5. 2: S on a C
6. 5: T on a F
7. 1: P in a PT
8. 7: D in a W

9. 1: N on a F
10. 2: W on a B
11. 10: Y in a D
12. 10: F on 2 H

Can you make up some of your own for others to solve?

Number Challenge ▼ → ★

Write down these numbers: 1 2 3 4 5 6 7 8 9

Without rearranging the order, make them total 100.

The only mathematical signs you are allowed to use

are pluses (+) and minuses (–).

Can you think of a way to make them total 50?

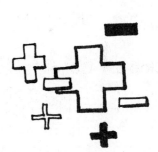

Sam's Multiplication ▼ → ★

Sam worked out that eight nines equal 1,125.

He proved to his teacher that he was right.

How did he do it?

Creative Thinking for Math

CREATIVE
THINKING
Math
TASK CARDS

Symbol Sum   → ★ ▼

Each symbol represents a number in the problem below.

Can you solve the sum?

```
    6 ◆ ●
    ■ ▲ 7
    3 5 ◆
  ‾‾●‾▲‾■‾
  ● 6 6 ■
```

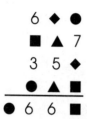

Fibonacci Numbers   → ★ ▼

Look at these numbers. They are all in a family called
Fibonacci numbers. They have a rule that allows them to belong to this
family.

Can you work out the rule to fill in all the blanks?

___, ___, ___, 3 , 5 , 8 , 13 , 21, ___, ___, ___, ___, ___, ___,

What is the rule?

Fibonacci numbers occur in nature: in pine cones, pineapples, and the petals of
many flowers. How many examples can you find that follow this sequence?

Counting Frames   → ★ ▼

On the planet Zup a counting frame is used where:
each bead on the first wire = 1
each bead on the second wire = 3
each bead on the third wire = 9
each bead on the fourth wire = 27
Thus, the number represented on this frame is _____
Draw counting frames showing these numbers: (a) 6   (b) 12   (c) 15   (d) 32   (e) 40
Make up your own number systems and give them to others to solve.

Creative Thinking for Science

Theme: Outer Space

Fluency

- Brainstorm words about outer space.
- Ask: "What is the difference between astronomy and astrology?"
- Have students list all the planets in our solar system.
- Ask: "What do you know about Mars/Meteorites/UFOs?"
- Say: "The answer is Jupiter. What are ten questions?"
- Have students list what they know about the Milky Way.
- Ask: "Which planets in our solar system have moons?"
- Make a large concept map of space and list questions for investigation.

Flexibility

- Have students think of as many categories as they can in which to group the words about space. Start them off with suggestions such as big and little, near and far.
- Ask: "Why do you think observatories are usually built in remote regions?"
- Ask students to group the planets in our solar system: (a) according to size (b) according to distance from the sun. Have them make a model.
- List all the advantages and disadvantages of space travel.
- Have students imagine that Earth was no longer able to sustain human life. List the things which could have happened to create this catastrophe.
- Say: "A manned Space Exploration Flight to Mars has been planned for the Year 2019. Give reasons why you think you should be on board."

Originality

- Ask: "What does Jupiter sound like?"

- Have students design an experiment which would test their reactions to weightlessness.
- Ask students to invent a solar-powered potted plant waterer.
- Say: "Imagine that you are the first to discover a new planet in our solar system beyond Pluto. What are you going to call it? Describe its shape, size, and unique characteristics."
- Have students experiment with different ways of launching a miniature UFO, using a piece of cardboard, five straws, and a rubber band.
- Challenge students to find a new way to prove that the world is not flat.

Elaboration

- Ask students to predict how people may change in the future as a result of space travel.
- Say: "Improve on the design of an existing spaceship. Bear in mind that spaceships of the future will be required to carry hundreds of people. They will also have to be very fast and extremely comfortable."
- Have students plan ten questions to ask a visitor from another planet which they consider will tell them all the important facts about life on that planet.
- Ask: "What might the consequences be if Earth's gravity decreased?"
- Select a product used in your home and redesign it so it can be used for space travel.
- Ask: "What would happen if the Earth moved 5,000 kms closer to the sun?"
- Have students create a model showing the differences between the landscapes on Mars and Earth.
- Ask: "How are other suns the same as ours? How are they different?"

Name:

Management
Strategies:

Solar System

On the chart below all the planets in our solar system are listed in order of their proximity to the sun. Fill in the squares with Yes or No. Some of the headings have been filled in for you. Use your own ideas for the rest.

Planet	Small	Round	Has moons		
Mercury					
Venus					
Earth					
Mars					
Jupiter					
Saturn					
Uranus					
Neptune					
Pluto					

What do all the planets have in common? _____

_____

In what ways are the planets different? _____

_____

What do Mercury, Venus, and Pluto have in common? _____

_____

List the planets according to their size._____

_____

Name:

Management
Strategies:

CREATIVE
THINKING

Science

BLM 20

Space Invention

Invent something unusual that can be used in space.

Suggestions: a feeding machine which can be used in a weightless environment, an alien-greeting robot, a space probe that can be sent out to analyze each new planet you approach

Describe your invention in the squares below.

What it is	Description of components
How it works	**What it can be used for**
Special features	**Illustration**

Creative Thinking for Social Studies

Theme: Pyramids of Egypt

Fluency

- Ask: "Can you name the Seven Wonders of the Ancient World? Where were they located?"
- Show the locations of the Seven Wonders on a map of the world.
- Ask students if they know why pyramids were built.
- Have students list the types of items discovered in Egyptian pyramids.
- Create a word bank of pyramid words.

Flexibility

- Say: "Of all the Seven Wonders of the Ancient World, the only one that remains today is the Great Pyramid. What do you think could be the reason(s) for this? How could some of the other structures have been preserved?"
- Compare the dimensions of the Great Pyramid to the school building and discuss similarities and differences.
- Have students list ten questions they could ask if they were interviewing one of the citizens of ancient Egypt.

Originality

- Ask students to brainstorm other uses for pyramids.
- Have students imagine that they are on an archaeological dig and have made an amazing discovery in one of the Egyptian pyramids. Ask them to describe what it is and why it is so incredible.
- Ask students to imagine they have found a time capsule from the time of the ancient Egyptians. Have them describe what items are contained within it.

Elaboration

- Have students check library sources or search the Internet to find the styles and intricate patterns of the Egyptian friezes which depicted life in ancient Egypt. Have them create their own frieze to display.
- Have students work in groups to demonstrate how pyramids were built, either by building a model, creating a play, or designing a chart. Ask them to improve on the original Egyptian design by making it more efficient.
- Have students research ancient Egyptian writing. Ask them to invent their own ancient style of writing and write a message which could have been left on the wall of an Egyptian pyramid.
- Have students research King Tut. Ask them to write a book entitled "The Secrets of Tut's Tomb." Ask them to imagine what topics this book could cover.
- Ask students to work in groups to tell the story of the discovery of Tut's tomb. Have them use music and sound effects to create suspense.
- Have students design a travel brochure about a tour of the Egyptian pyramids.

Name: _____

CREATIVE THINKING
Social Studies
BLM 21

Pyramids of Egypt

To the right is a drawing of an Egyptian pyramid.

The purpose of the Egyptian pyramid was _____

_____

Substitute something on the pyramid: _____

Combine it with something else: _____

Adapt it to make it suitable for another purpose: _____

Modify the size: _____

Divide it into **Portions**: _____

Eliminate part of it: _____

Reverse it: _____

After you have written in your ideas for the changes to the Egyptian pyramid, draw your own version. Label all the changes you have made.

My new design is called _____

Its purpose is _____

Name:

Management
Strategies:

Egyptian Writing

If you visit Egypt, you may find some very old writing on some walls. Here is what some of the symbols mean:

reeds   water   boat   sun   good health   food   house

What do you think this says?

My interpretation _____

_____

_____

_____

Now design your own picture alphabet, which tells a story about life in ancient Egypt and the building of the Great Pyramid. When you have finished, give it to a friend to see if they can interpret your story.

My Picture Alphabet Symbols

My Story

Solutions to BLMS and Task Cards

(Please note that those questions with open-ended responses do not have solutions below.)

Cryptic Numbers (p. 51)

1. 2 eyes in a head
2. 4 seasons in a year
3. 12 days of Christmas
4. 4 legs on a dog
5. 2 sides on a coin
6. 5 toes on a foot
7. 1 partridge in a pear tree
8. 7 days in a week
9. 1 nose on a face
10. 2 wheels on a bike
11. 10 years in a decade
12. 10 fingers on 2 hands

Number Challenge (p. 51)

$123 + 45 - 67 + 8 - 9 = 100$

Sam's Multiplication (p. 51)

$9 + 9 + 9 + 99 + 999 = 1125$

Symbol Sum (p. 52)

♦ = 2   ● = 1   ■ = 4   ▲ = 9

Fibonacci Numbers (p. 52)

1, 1, 2, 3, 5, 8, 13, 21, 34, 55, 89, 144, 233, 377

Counting Frames (p. 52)

162

Research
Skills
Notes and Activities

by Rosalind Curtis

Overview for the
Classroom Teacher

Research Skills

Research skills are needed by all students so that they can analyze and interpret information that is presented to them. Information can be presented to students by means of written text, visual input (pictures, videos, computer terminal), aural input (listening to speakers, radio, sounds within the environment), and kinesthetic input (senses of touch, taste, and smell).

Research skills that need to be taught to students:

Questioning techniques help students clarify issues, solve problems, and make decisions when looking at a topic.

Developing planning frameworks will assist students to access prior knowledge and identify sources of information which will help build further knowledge and understanding.

Gathering strategies helps students collect and store information for later consideration, for example, note-taking, identifying main ideas, and text clarification.

Sorting strategies helps students to prioritize and organize information by using retrieval charts and sequencing information, for example.

Synthesizing skills helps students take the original information and reorganize it in order to develop decisions and solutions.

Evaluation helps the students to determine if the information found is sufficient to support a solution or conclusion.

Reporting skills allow the students to translate findings into persuasive, instructive, and effective products, for example, in the presentation of a project.

These research skills are best taught within the classroom by means of a **research cycle**. This cycle provides students with the steps to plan and conduct meaningful research to complete projects, solve problems, and make informed decisions.

① Students **explore** a variety of sources from which to gather information.

⑦ After completion of analysis, students will **combine** their findings to create their final projects.

② Students **identify** information sources that will contain data to help with their decisions.

⑥ Students **ask** themselves why this information is important and how it will affect their decisions.

③ Once information is found, **decisions** must be made about which data to keep.

⑤ Students begin to **analyze** their data by establishing criteria that will help them reach decisions.

④ Students **sort** information to enable them to categorize and organize their findings so that analysis can begin.

Overview for the Classroom Teacher

The Research Cycle

There are seven steps in the research cycle.

1. Questioning

- This step identifies the problem that needs solving.
- Students need to be taught questioning skills which will enable them to identify what data is needed to solve the main problem. It is critical students are encouraged to think laterally and from as many perspectives as possible.
- From the questioning process, students should be able to identify information they already know and formulate questions to locate information they need to find out.

2. Planning

- This step begins to develop information-seeking strategies to help locate answers to all the questions asked.
- Students need to be introduced to the range of resources which are available, such as books, videos, people, pictures, and the Internet.
- Students need to plan how to organize the information that will be gathered.

3. Gathering

- This step enables students to clarify the information that has been located.
- Students need to develop effective note-taking strategies so that the main idea is identified from the information.
- Students also need to recognize the value of a bibliography so that they can return to it as an information source if required.

4. Sorting

- This step requires students to systematically scan the data for relevant information that will contribute to understanding.
- Students need to classify the gathered information under headings and sub-headings and make generalizations about it.
- The data gathered can then be placed into a sequence of events.

5. Synthesizing

- This process is like doing a jigsaw puzzle.
- Students need to arrange and rearrange fragments of information until patterns begin to emerge.
- Students develop their skills so that they are able to answer questions with understanding, accuracy, and detail.

6. Evaluation

- When this stage is first reached, early attempts to synthesize information may result in the need for more information to clarify or enhance understanding. If the students find that pieces are missing, they will need to begin the cycle again or ask what more is needed to complete the picture.
- As the cycle begins again, questioning will become more specific and will lead to more planning and more gathering of information.
- When the picture seems to be complete, the students can decide that the cycle should finish.
- It may be necessary to repeat the cycle and gather more information until the students decide that an investigation is complete.

7. Reporting

- After the cycle has been completed, it is time to report and share findings. This may take the form of an oral, written, or graphic presentation, a debate, or any other presentation that students may decide upon.

Classroom Design

- Have students work independently or in mixed ability or homogeneous groups, as appropriate for the activity.
- Provide a variety of resources around the room, including hands-on and extension activities and learning centers aimed at different levels.
- Always give criteria for evaluation and a time line for work to be completed.

Research Skills for English

Theme: Koalas

Questioning

- Ask a range of questions about the koala which progressively become more difficult:
  - What sort of animal is a Koala? Where would I find it? What does it look like? What does it eat? What are some dangers it faces?
- Encourage students to formulate their own questions.

Planning

- Ask students to list all that they know about the koala.
- Have students identify facts or information they would like to find out about the koala, for example, how to preserve its habitat.
- Have students identify likely sources of information which will assist them.

Gathering

- Present written information on koalas and have students identify key words by underlining them.
- Have students read books on koalas and take notes.
- Have students suggest words that could be used to search the Internet for information on koalas. Place this list of words on the classroom wall. Develop subtopics to refine searches, for example habitat—gum trees, eucalyptus forests, etc.

Sorting

- Ask students to group information under headings like: Description, Habitat, Dangers, Habits.
- Have students group statements according to common elements and then into time lines or sequential order.

Synthesizing

- Have students watch a video related to koalas and devise questions for other students to answer.
- Show a picture to the students of a

forest being cut down. Have students come up with the types of problems that this could create for the koala.
- Have students access web sites such as:
  www.schoolworld.asn.au/species/koala
  and
  http//akfkoala.gil.com.au/koala.html.
  Ask students to summarize important facts from these web sites. Have students prepare a report to submit to the web site.

Evaluating

- Have students try to convince a friend that koalas are special animals and need to have their habitat preserved.
- Ask students to write a letter to the local newspaper in support of the "Save the Koala" fund.
- Give students some statements about koalas that are incorrect and have the students correct them.

Reporting

- Have students present an oral report explaining why koalas are on the endangered list.
- Have students work in groups of four to present a play depicting the plight of a koala whose habitat is endangered.
- Ask students to debate the topic: "A koala's habitat is more important than urban development."

Name:

Koalas

Make these statements into questions.

Factual

1. Koalas, kangaroos, dolphins, and humans are all types of mammals.

_____

_____

Inferential

2. With more houses being built and more families moving into the area, more domestic animals will be a part of a koala's habitat.

_____

_____

Critical

3. I think that we need to stop allowing houses to be built in the habitat of koalas.

_____

_____

Creative

4. Sometimes a koala can "fly" from a limb of one tree to a limb of another.

_____

_____

Factual

_____

_____

_____

Inferential

_____

_____

Critical

_____

_____

_____

Creative

_____

_____

Devise four questions of your own about the koala.

Name: _____

Traveling Overseas

Management
Strategies:

❖ ⇛ ●

Gathering, Sorting,
Analyzing

RESEARCH
SKILLS
English
BLM 24

1. List the things you would need to organize before leaving the United States to go on an overseas trip.

   _____   _____

   _____   _____

   _____   _____

   _____   _____

   _____   _____

   _____   _____

2. Where would you locate information about the length and cost of an overseas trip?

   _____

   _____

   _____

   _____

   _____

3. What are some of the problems you could encounter? How would you avoid these problems?

   Problem   **How to avoid it**

   _____   _____

   _____   _____

   _____   _____

   _____   _____

   _____   _____

   _____   _____

   _____   _____

Research Skills for English

Evaluation

▼ → ⇒ ✖

Improving Transportion

Choose one form of transportion. Improve this form of transportion so that it can move more people than it presently does and would be more comfortable for a long trip.

Draw your new form of transportation and describe the improvements you have made.

▼ → ⇒ ✖

Alternatives

Find ten different uses for a helicopter.

▼ → ⇒ ✖

Runaway Train

How could you stop a runaway train by using

- fishing net?
- a water pistol?
- scissors?

▼ → ⇒ ✖

Public Transportion

People don't like using public transportion.

Brainstorm solutions.

Research Skills for English

Synthesizing

▼ → ⇒

Snow for Sale

Think of some innovative uses for snow.

Design an advertising campaign to sell snow.

▼ → ⇒

Snow Machine

Combine the attributes of a space rocket control panel and a lawn mower to design something that can be used in the snow.

▼ → ⇒

Explanations

Bright purple snow is falling!

Give five possible explanations for this.

▼ → ⇒

Mount Everest

Consider this statement:

"Everyone should be banned from climbing Mount Everest."

What do you think?

Research Skills for Math

Theme: Surveys

Questioning

- Ensure that students understand the language associated with surveys. For example: 'What type of questions elicit the desired responses for a survey?'

- Have students look at survey answers represented in different forms (graphs, percentages, statements). Ask them to work with a partner to devise questions for these. Examples follow:

  Statement: Most students have brown eyes. Question: Which color eyes do you have?

- Ask students to devise survey questions relating to preferences that have only two possible answers. For example: "Is your favorite color orange or green?"

Planning

- Have students draw a picture for each category of their survey.

- Have students predict what they think the survey outcome will be.

- Have students list those people they think they should interview. On what criteria were the people chosen? Will this limit the results of the survey?

Gathering

- Conduct surveys on a variety of topics such as what sort of food students eat for their lunch or what types of cars their parents drive.

- Have students tally responses in a variety of different ways (pictures, tally marks, circles).

Sorting

- Have students sort their collected data into different categories, for example: All students who like cheese sandwiches.

- If students chart their results have them determine what is included on each axis of a line graph or on each part of a pie graph. For example: x axis = number of pies eaten and y axis = types of pies eaten.

Synthesizing

- Prepare challenge cards that require students to apply math within real-life situations. For example: Which food should the school cafeteria buy more of? Why?

- Ask students to interpret information from graphs and to make comparative statements such as: "There were more wet days in March than dry days."

- Have students represent their findings in a variety of graph forms.

Evaluating

- Ask students to interpret data from a graph that is presented to them.

- Have students explain why their predictions for survey responses were close to or far from the actual answers.

- Have students make generalizations about their findings, for example, more people eat *Wheaties* than *Fruit Loops*.

- Ask students to decide how they could rephrase a question if it did not provide the desired data.

Reporting

- Have students summarize and present their findings from surveys that they have conducted.

- Encourage students to use a variety of means to present their findings visually as bar graphs, picture graphs, and models.

Name:

Management
Strategies:

● ▼ ❖

RESEARCH
SKILLS

Math

BLM 25

Survey

You have been asked by the school cafeteria to find out which food items are the most popular.

Write down four survey questions to find out this information.

Question 1

_____
_____
_____
_____

Question 2

_____
_____
_____
_____

Question 3

_____
_____
_____
_____

Question 4

_____
_____
_____
_____

Complete the survey with 10 or 20 people and present the information in graph form. You may use a bar graph, pie graph, line graph, or picture graph.

Name:

Tesselations

1. On a separate sheet of paper, draw an equilateral triangle with sides of 2 inches (5cm). (See 1.)

2. Modify the triangle by cutting into one side and removing a piece. (See 2.)

3. Transfer this piece to the opposite side of the triangle and re-attach it. (See 3.)

4. Modify the last side of the triangle by cutting out a small piece. Re-attach the cutout piece to that side of the triangle. (See 4.)

5. On a separate sheet of paper make a tessellation with this new shape.

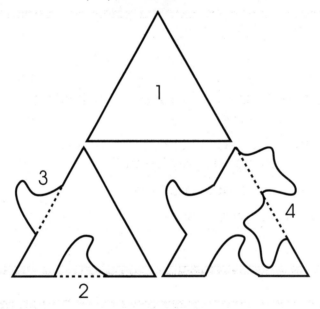

EXTENSION:

Write your own instructions for how to create a tesselation and give them to your friend to follow.

_____

_____

_____

_____

_____

Research Skills for Math

Evaluating and Synthesizing

Survey Findings

❖ ● ▼

Step 1: Interview three people.

Step 2: The questions you ask of them are to be related to advertising.

Step 3: You must discover what type of advertising these people prefer and what type they do not prefer.

Step 4: Present your findings visually.

Estimation

❖ ● ▼

Step 1: Estimate how many jelly beans would fit into a one quart container.

Step 2: How could you check your answer without actually counting the jelly beans?

Step 3: Would this be a reliable method?

Step 4: Give reasons for your answer.

Different Ways

❖ ● ▼

How many different ways can you get the correct answer?

I throw a dice ten times.
The total number I throw is **47.**

What numbers could I have thrown to arrive at this number?

Research Skills for Math

Evaluation and Synthesizing

Measuring the Oval

Step 1: You have to determine the perimeter of the oval. There are no wheels, tape measures, or rulers available to accurately measure the oval.

Step 2: How would you measure the oval?

Step 3: What would you use as a measuring tool?

Step 4: How would you convert your measurement to yards?

Fun Run

Use a local map to plan a fun run. The run has to

- be no longer than 10 kilometers
- start and finish at the school
- cross more than 5 roads

Draw your fun run, detailing landmarks, the streets, and directions given to the runners before they begin.

Weighing

Step 1: You have been given a box with measurements of **40** cm long by **60** cm wide and **10** cm high. You need to determine how much it would weigh if you were to fill it with sand. The only measuring tool you have is an old set of kitchen scales that weigh up to **750** grams. Explain how you would use this set of scales to determine the weight of the full box.

Step 2: What other ways could you think of to determine the weight of the full box of sand?

Research Skills for Science

Theme: Solar System

Questioning

- Have students write down questions about the solar system that they would like to find answers to:
  - Which planet looks the brightest in the night sky? Who discovered and named Pluto? Where can we find out more information about our solar system?
- Have students identify elements needed to sustain life on Earth by asking questions:
  - What would happen if the sun could not be seen at all? Why do plants need water? How do we rely on plants and animals?

Planning

- Ask students to make predictions about what they think would happen if an asteroid hit Earth.
- Have students identify a hypothesis relating to a feature of the solar system that they think would affect Earth in some way. For example: "If the night sky was cloudy, how would this affect the navigation of nineteenth-century sailing ships?"

Gathering

- Have students track the paths of stars and planets over a period of time.
- Have students consult past records of planets or star positions for a specific time each year and compare it with the present position. Record the date, season and month. Compare and contrast results.
- Have students identify scientific concepts of observation, hypothesizing, and generalizing relating to different elements of the solar system.
  (a) Observation: Watching and recording phases of the moon.
  (b) Hypothesizing: The planets will return to the same position in the sky at set intervals.

(c) Generalizing: Comets have set paths that they follow around the sun, as do planets.

Sorting

- Have students sort various items according to different attributes. For example, planets could be sorted into large and small.
- Have students verbalize observations in terms of cause and effect. For example, the moon circling the Earth determines our tides.
- Ask students to categorize elements for sustaining life into human-controlled and nature-controlled elements.
- Have students organize the procedures followed to carry out an experiment in the correct sequence such as investigating the effect of gravity on satellites orbiting Earth.

Synthesizing

- Have students design and build models of our own and a "new" solar system.
- Have students write a letter to the editor about the effects of space junk on our solar system.
- Using the laws of probability and past records, have students predict the path of Halley's Comet in 2056.

Evaluating

- Have students devise ways to maintain life after a nuclear holocaust or when colonizing another planet.
- Ask students to explain why their new planetary system could sustain life.
- Have students describe the attributes of planets that make them belong to a specific group, for example, planets with moons.

Reporting

- Have a science fest where students exhibit a project relating to our solar system, one they have devised and carried out.

Name:

Solar System

TASK 1: Work in groups of 4 to become experts on one of the following:

moon	satellite	black hole
sun	planet	star constellation
asteroid	comet	

Each member of the group must write down the information that is gathered. Use this space to make your notes.

My group became an expert on _____

Key Facts

_____   _____

_____   _____

_____   _____

_____   _____

_____

TASK 2: Join with an expert from each of the other groups. Share your information about your member of the solar system.

TASK 3: Within your new group, combine all the objects you have described to form a new solar system. Give the system a

name. Make a sketch of what the solar system would look like.

TASK 4: Make a diorama to display your new system. Label all parts of

Research Skills for Social Studies

Theme: Survival

Questioning

- Have students identify what they already know about survival.

- Prepare questions for students to answer which will encourage them to think about survival skills. Examples:
  - What do I need to survive? (factual)
  - What does survival mean? (factual)
  - How do I ensure that I have everything I need to survive? (inferential)
  - If I had to do without something to survive, what would it be? (critical)
  - If I could add another element to my needs for survival, what would it be? (creative)

Planning

- List resources that could be used to find information about survival:
  - non-fiction books relating to the human body or survival techniques
  - fiction books such as *Robinson Crusoe* or *Swiss Family Robinson*
  - the Internet
  - biographies of people who have survived after airplane crashes or shipwrecks
- Have students develop a mind map to help with their storing of information.
- Have students identify what they need to find out about survival.

Gathering

- Have students read extracts from fiction that detail how people survived after shipwrecks or being lost in the wilderness.
- Have students identify keywords from texts that relate to survival. This could form the basis of a survival handbook.
- Show videos such as *Swiss Family Robinson*. Ask students to write down ways that the family survived.

Sorting

- Ask students to compile their notes into lists of things that you can use from nature to survive and artificial things that have been developed by people to survive.
- Have students divide their information into cause and effect, for example: "The storm caused the ship to sink. The effect was being isolated on a tropical island."

Synthesizing

- Have students think of all the ways they can use a piece of rope, a sheet, and a bucket to help them gather food and retrieve things from the ship.
- Ask students to think of things they would need to do to make life bearable until they are rescued.

Evaluating

- Have students list three people they would like to be shipwrecked with and to give reasons for their choices.
- Ask students to list things they would need to retrieve from the ship to help in their survival.

Reporting

- Have students keep a log of their stay on the island, detailing how they spent their time.
- Ask students to role-play their rescue.
- Have students write a newspaper article detailing the rescue.

Name:

Survival Skills

Gathering, Synthesizing, Evaluating

You and a friend have been shipwrecked on a deserted island. The ship you were on has sunk in 400 feet(10 meters) of water not far from the shore. All that you could salvage as the ship sank were

- a piece of rope

- a sheet from one of the bunks

- a bucket

You must both survive until the next ship passes in 30 days.

List the additional things you would try to salvage from the sunken ship.

_____

_____

_____

How would you salvage these items?

_____

_____

_____

Describe what you would do to survive.

_____

_____

_____

_____

Invent something that would help you to attract the attention of the passing ship. Describe and illustrate how this would help you.

_____

_____

_____

_____

_____

Research Skills for Creative Arts

Theme: Designing an Exhibit for the Local Museum

Questioning

- Post the question: "How many different types of museums are there?"
- Ask students to list what they would find at a museum.
- Have students clarify vocabulary like artifacts, hieroglyphs, excavations.
- Have students identify things they would like to know about museums and displays:
  - Where is my nearest museum?
  - What items would be suitable to display at this museum?
  - Who could I talk to about setting up a display?
  - What steps do I need to take to set up a display?

Planning

- Have students plan what they would like to exhibit.
- Ask students to list resources that could be used to locate information for designing and planning their exhibit. For example: the Internet, encyclopedias, local museum.
- Have students make a list of questions for data they need to locate.
- Model a mind map, then have students devise their own, using the questions they have listed.
- Ask students to think about timelines for the items they are exhibiting.

Gathering

- Have students visit a local museum to observe ways that exhibits are presented.
- Have students identify indicators for determining the age of artifacts from videos and written texts.
- Ask students to write down key facts about the world of 2000 years ago.

Sorting

- Have students organize their data about artifacts into a timeline.
- Ask students to list the things that would have been used 2000 years ago, such as clay pots, statues and gold jewelry.
- Have students sort information about artifacts into various categories. For example: Household Items or Valuable Items.

Synthesizing

- Have students write a description of an exhibit they saw at the museum.
- Ask students to identify problems that could arise with their exhibit.
- Have students design a poster advertising the exhibition.

Evaluating

- Have students evaluate an exhibition they have seen.
- Have students design the layout for their exhibit, showing where each item will be placed.
- Have students design the display according to chronological order, or artifacts made from the same material, or found in the same area. Ask them to explain their reason for choosing this style of display.

Reporting

- Have students make a model of their display.
- Ask students to write a report for the newspaper critiquing the display.

Name:

Designing an Exhibit

You have been asked to design a new exhibit for the local museum, one containing artifacts found during the excavations of a city believed to be over 2,000 years old. How would you choose what to display and what information to provide for visitors?

Use this sheet to jot down your findings and to begin your preliminary sketches of the exhibit. Include some drawings of artifacts that will be on display.

List of artifacts chosen for display	Information about the artifacts

Plan of display

Make Your Own Task Cards

Questioning and Brainstorming Skills

Notes and Activities

by Rosalind Curtis

Overview for the Classroom Teacher

Questioning

Generally speaking, 30% of class time is taken up in questioning (that is about 100 questions per hour). In most classrooms 85% of questions are asked by the teacher, and 90% of those do no more than demand memory or recall by the students! Therefore, teachers should aim to use more open-ended and divergent questions to improve the students' creative thinking and problem solving abilities.

Questioning Guidelines for the Teacher:

1. Maintain a high level of enthusiasm.
2. Accept that individual differences in students will determine how, what, how much, how fast learning occurs.
3. Encourage divergent thinking.
4. Avoid all forms of negative comments. Be positive! "Great!" "Good try!" "Tell me more!" "I've never thought of it like that!"
5. Try to minimize "Who?" "What?" "Where?" and maximize "Why?" "How?"

Bloom's Taxonomy emphasizes the idea that with brighter students, more time should be devoted to the higher level activities and objectives. Knowledge and comprehension deal with facts, figures, definitions, and rules which all students need to know. However, teachers should encourage the brighter students (who will generally grasp new information quickly and comprehend more rapidly) to

- *apply* this knowledge;
- *analyze* components, relationships, and hypotheses;
- *synthesize* these components into creative solutions, plans, and theories;
- *evaluate* the accuracy, value, and efficiency of alternative ideas or actions.

Examples of questions which help to apply knowledge:

When did...?
Can you list...?
Which action/event was the cause of...?
Can you give an example of...?
How would you have...?
Why was...?

Examples of questions which help to analyze knowledge:

Why did...do this?
Can you sequence...?

Examples of questions which help to synthesize knowledge:

How would this situation have changed if...?
What if the "bears" had been "monkeys"?

Examples of questions which help to evaluate the knowledge:

How could ... have been improved?
Who do you think has the strongest character? Why?

Overview for the Classroom Teacher

Brainstorming

Another technique which encourages creative thinking is **brainstorming**.

The aim of brainstorming is to develop a safe, non-judgmental setting where all students feel confident and eager to participate in the lesson.

It was Alex Osborn who identified some valuable conditions and rules for brainstorming. The main principle is deferred judgment. This means that idea evaluation is postponed until later. Osborn stressed that any kind of criticism or evaluation interferes with the generation of imaginative ideas simply because it is very difficult to do both at the same time.

It is important for the teacher to remind the students of the basic rules of brainstorming:

1. No criticism is allowed no matter how irrelevant or preposterous the responses may appear to be.

2. A large quantity of ideas is required. The more ideas you have, the more likely it is that you will have motivated all students to contribute, and thus it is more likely that you will find good solutions.

3. Accept and record all answers. To begin with, it is perhaps easier for the teacher to be the scribe, but when brainstorming is a regular feature of the class's activities, students can record responses.

4. Eliminate any stiffness or inflexibility. Be open to alternatives.

5. If responses slack off, add your own. The teacher's role is to keep urging: "What else could we do? Who else has an idea?" The teacher may even specifically direct questions to a group of quieter students.

6. Link ideas wherever possible. Ask questions such as "How can we express this more clearly?" "Could we improve this one?" "What if we put these three ideas together?"

7. Encourage fantasy, imagination, and lateral thinking.

8. Encourage cooperative work among students.

9. If there were a school problem (for example, the sudden appearance of graffiti on the school playground), the students could be given 24-hours notice so that all have an opportunity to discuss this at home and can be prepared to brainstorm a solution for the next day. Brighter students soon learn to organize and lead group brainstorming sessions.

Some variations of brainstorming:

Reverse Brainstorming: This technique quickly points out what is currently being done incorrectly and implicitly suggests specific solutions. For example, how can we increase vandalism?

"Stop-and-Go" Brainstorming: Short periods of approximately 6 – 8 minutes of brainstorming are interspersed with evaluation. The evaluation sheets help keep the group on target by selecting the most profitable directions to pursue.

Phillips 66: This is a technique using small groups of 6. Students brainstorm for 6 minutes and then a member of each group reports the best, or all, ideas to the larger group.

Questioning and Brainstorming Skills for English

Theme: Heroes and Heroines

Knowledge

- Explain that the word "hero" will be used to refer to both males and females.

- Brainstorm: "What makes a person a hero?"

- Ask students: "Can you write a definition of a hero?"

- Pose the question: "Are there any particular occupations from which 'heroes' emerge? Why do you think this is so?"

Comprehension

Pose these questions:

- Can you provide some examples of heroes? What did these people do to become heroes?

- Do all heroes fit a certain physical stereotype? For example, are they all tall, strong, and athletic?

- Does a hero have to be a human being? Why? Why not?

- Challenge students to devise a sequence of questions to determine if someone/something is a hero.

Application

Brainstorm for answers:

- Who were some heroes from history? (Include examples from different areas such as Florence Nightingale, Burke and Wills, and Jesse Owens.)

- Why are these people remembered as heroes?

- Who are some heroes from fictional stories or movies? Why are they considered heroes?

- Which people were heroes in the 1998 Sydney to Hobart Yacht Race? Why?

- Do you think you have the qualities to be a hero? Why/Why not?

Analysis

- Have the students list all the ways that people in the following occupations could be heroes:

  (a) teachers   (b) doctors

  (c) plumbers   (d) nurses

  (e) bank tellers   (f) students

  (g) bus drivers

- Brainstorm the answers: "Why are soldiers often thought of as heroes? Why are medals or commendations given to many of them?"

Synthesis

- Have the students work in groups of 3 or 4 to list all the ways that they could become heroes.

- Say: "If you were able to interview one of the heroes you have named, who would you choose? Why? List five questions you would like to ask."

- Ask: "Do you think that heroes are ever afraid? Why? Why not? If yes, then what might they be afraid of?"

Evaluation

- Pose the question: "What is admired most about a hero?"

- Ask: "How can we best let a person know if we think that person is a hero?"

- Have the students work in small groups of 4 or 5 to list the ten most important qualities they think a hero should possess. Then have students revisit the questions they devised for "Comprehension" to determine whether someone/something was a hero. Are the questions sufficient?

- Ask students to write a report about someone they know personally who might be considered a hero.

Questioning and Brainstorming Skills for English

Knowledge, Comprehension, Application, Analysis

Nicknames

What are the nicknames of these famous people? Why do you think they were given them?

Florence Nightingale

Tony Locket

Sir Edward Dunlop

Joan Sutherland

Margaret Thatcher

Greg Norman

Erwin Rommell

The Duke of Wellington

Favorite Heroes

Work with a partner to list your ten favorite heroes.

State which field they are from and why you chose them.

Humanitarian Heroes

Work in groups of 3 or 4. Choose one or more of these humanitarian heroes to research. Write reports which highlight some of the ways they have helped people.

Mother Theresa

Mahatma Gandhi

Martin Luther King, Jr.

Albert Schweitzer

William Wilberforce

Daisy Bates

Book Heroes

Name some of the heroes created by these writers:

Henry Lawson

Colleen McCullough

Colin Thiele

Robin Klein

Beatrix Potter

Robert Louis Stevenson

Charles Dickens

Ethel Turner

Paul Jennings

Questioning and Brainstorming Skills for English

Analysis, Synthesis, Evaluation

Non-Human Hero

Suggest a scenario where a non-human becomes a hero.

Cartoon Hero

Who is your favorite cartoon hero?

Draw him/her in action.

My Hero

From all the people you have ever known, read about, or heard about, choose the one person who impresses you most.

Write a haiku or limerick about this person.

My Turn to Be a Hero

Write the letters A–Z down one side of your page. For each letter think of a situation in which you could become a hero. Example:

Avalanche—I could help rescue someone from beneath the snow.

Name:

Management Strategies:

Heroes

Synthesis

Imagine you have the opportunity to become a hero.

Choose one of these scenarios:
- a fire
- an accident
- a storm

Display your heroic feats in this cartoon strip.

1	2	3
4	**5**	**6**
7	**8**	**9**

Name:

Heroes

Management
Strategies:

Analysis, Synthesis, Evaluation

QUESTION/
BRAINSTORM

English

BLM 31

What can you find out about each of these heroes?

Write a short description of their accomplishments, and select one other hero in their field of excellence.

Medicine	Sports	Defense Forces
Victor Chang	**Susie O'Neill**	**Sir Edward Dunlop**
Another hero is	Another hero is	Another hero is

Humanitarian	Writing	Music
Carolyn Chisholm	**Oodgeroo Noonuccal**	**David Helfgott**
Another hero is	Another hero is	Another hero is

Questioning and Brainstorming Skills for Math

Theme: Time

Knowledge
- Brainstorm: Why do people need to know the time of day/week/month/year?
- Brainstorm different ways of telling the time. For example, 7:15 could also be expressed as: (a) 15 minutes past 7, (b) a quarter past seven, or (c) 07:15 (A.M.) or 19:15 (P.M.).
- Find out what students know about the new Internet time.

Comprehension
- Ask students to research how our ancestors told the time of day and year, for example, the sun dial. Ask them if some people still use these methods.
- Pose thee questions: When did the first clocks appear? What form did these early clocks take?
- Ask: When were the first watches invented?
- Have students describe how they think clocks or digital watches work.

Application
- Give students copies of various time tables (bus, train, airplane) and pose questions about them. For example: If you lived in Perth and wanted to arrive in Brisbane in time for a meeting at 10 a.m. on Wednesday, which flight would you have to catch?
- Ask: What are some occasions when people depend on knowing the correct time?
- Provide students with a cardboard replica of an ordinary clock face and have them fill in a second circle of numbers to produce a 24 hour clock face.
- Ask students where 24-hour time is commonly used. Have them provide reasons for this.
- Have each student select a number between 0 and 99. Ask them to create a time line of events that occurred in that year of each century. For example, if they select 60, they could choose:

1960—John F. Kennedy became president of the United States; 1860—Lister pioneered work on antiseptic surgery; 1760—George III became King of England. Make sure that each student chooses a different number, and display the results of their work around the classroom.

Analysis
- Have students list as many early "time tellers" as they can. Ask: In what ways were these early time pieces not always satisfactory?
- Challenge students to name as many present-day time indicators as they can. Have them select those used for very short as well as very long time spans.
- Ask: Why do we need such a variety of instruments to tell the time?
- Have students research where these time indicators can be found, for example, in a family home or in a special establishment.

Synthesis
- Pose questions about time zones for students to investigate:
  - Why are times in New York different from times in Chicago and Los Angeles?
  - When we watch sports such as tennis being televised live from England, why are we watching them at night, when they are being played in the morning or afternoon?
  - Where is the International Date Line? What is its importance?
  - What is Greenwich Mean Time? Where is Greenwich?

Evaluation
- Investigate some feelings about daylight saving, by asking:
  - What is daylight saving? When do we use it? Why do we use it? Do you think it is a good or bad thing? Why?

Questioning and Brainstorming Skills for Math

Comprehension, Application, Analysis

▼ ✱ ✖

Estimation

Estimate how long it would take to do each of the following, and then record the actual time taken:

Print your first name.

Count out one dollar in 5-cent pieces.

Walk 50 yards.

Tie your shoelaces.

Run around the school.

Hand out a book to each class member.

▼ ✱ ✖

Calculation

How many days, hours, and minutes from today until:

Christmas Day

Veterans' Day

You become 16

▼ ✱ ✖

Time Development

What effect did each of the following people have on the development of accurate time keeping?

- Julius Caesar

- Pope Gregory XIII

- John Harrison

▼ ✱ ✖

Graphing

Work with a partner. Time each other doing the following activities over 100 yards or meters and show your results in graph form. Use line, bar, pie, or picture graphs.

- running

- walking

- skipping

- walking backwards

Questioning and Brainstorming Skills for Math

Analysis, Synthesis, Evaluation

Timekeeping

Brainstorm new ways

for timing races.

Recording Dates

Research how dates are recorded in the following countries.

- Australia
- China
- Iran
- India

早上女子

Light Year

Write a mathematical story involving a light year.

International Date Line

Research the International Date Line.

Where is it?

Why is it necessary?

Which is the first place on Earth to celebrate the new year?

Name:

Management
Strategies:

Comprehension,
Application, Analysis

QUESTION/
BRAINSTORM

Math

BLM 32

Time Research Tasks

Illustrate the following time pieces and explain how each one operates.

Sun Dial

Description: _____

_____

_____

_____

Clepsydra

Description: _____

_____

_____

_____

Candle

Description: _____

_____

_____

_____

Caesium Atomic Clock

Description: _____

_____

_____

_____

Name: _____

Time Tasks

Task: 1: Explain the meanings of these time words:

Millennium _____

Olympiad _____

Lunar month _____

Calendar month _____

BCE _____

Solstice _____

Equinox _____

Task 2: Complete this pie graph to indicate how your day is spent at school. Show all your subjects, lunch, and recess breaks with the time each one takes.

Task 3: Draw a pie graph showing how your *ideal* day would be spent.

Questioning and Brainstorming Skills for Science

Theme: Food

Knowledge

Brainstorm:

- What is food?
- Who needs food?
- Why do we need food?
- What is your favorite food? (Record all responses and use this information for drawing up bar graphs, picture graphs, or pie graphs.)

Comprehension

Brainstorm:

- Why do we need variety in the food we eat?
- Why is breakfast known as "the most important meal of the day?"
- What is a dietician?

Application

- Ask each member of the class to keep a daily diary recording all foods consumed. Over a period of one week have students note what they eat and when.
- Invite a dietician to your school to speak to your class or grade about the following:
  - the food they should be eating
  - the food they should be reducing in their intake
  - why they should eat more of some foods and less of others
  - how often they should eat

Analysis

- Have students refer to the daily diary activity and divide their foods into ones that they should eat more of (apples) and ones that they should eat less of (potato chips).
- Brainstorm what students now understand to be a balanced diet. Have students devise a list of ten questions to determine whether someone has a balanced diet.

- Have students list the five main food groups and give examples of common foods in each group.
- Brainstorm: "What does the old saying 'You are what you eat' mean?"
- Analyze the types of foods sold from the school cafeteria. Draw up a pie graph of the most popular foods.

Synthesis

- Have students think of ways that they could improve the quality of their daily food intake.
- Have students work in groups to list the food commercials that have influenced them most. Then ask them to devise their own food commercials.
- Have students imagine that they are dieticians and ask them to devise answers to questions they could be asked by clients. Examples:
  - What is the best way for me to lose weight?
  - If I want to gain weight, should I just eat more?
  - Why are liquids such an important part of a food plan?

Evaluation

- Have students evaluate why food needs for adolescents are different from those of adults and different again from those of the elderly.
- Ask: Why do you think most children don't like vegetables? Can you think of a solution to this problem?
- Have students create a "good eating" diorama to display in the classroom, school library or cafeteria.

Name:

Management
Strategies:

Planning a Dinner Menu

Task 1: How many of your favorite foods originated in another country? Complete this table.

Country	Name of Dish	Main Ingredients
Italy		
Spain		
China		
India		

Task 2: On a separate sheet of paper, record your family's preferences for food from each country.

Use this information to plan a dinner menu for your family. Remember to include all five-food groups.

Print the menu for your gala dinner.

Special Family Menu

Appetizer/Soup/Salad:

Main Course:

Dessert:

Name:

Lunch Special

Management
Strategies:

Analysis, Synthesis,
Evaluation

QUESTION/
BRAINSTORM

Science

BLM 35

Task 1: Organize a "lunch special" for your school cafeteria. Make sure that, as well as being tasty, it is also healthy.

Describe and illustrate your meal in the box below.

Name of Lunch Special	Illustration
Description	
_____	
_____	
_____	
_____	
_____	

Task 2: Design and produce an advertising poster for your lunch special.

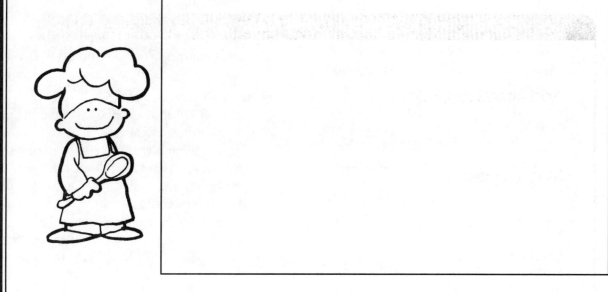

Questioning and Brainstorming Skills for Social Studies

Theme: Disasters Around the World

Knowledge

Involve the class in the stimulation of a discussion on disasters. Give the class five minutes to devise their own questions about disasters. Have one student read a question to the class to commence the discussion and then others, in turn, as it progresses. Some typical discussion questions may include these:

- Have you ever seen a disaster? Can you describe to the class what happened?
- How would you describe a disaster?
- What are some recent disasters?
- Where did these disasters take place?
- What are some other major disasters that have taken place throughout time?
- Would an airplane crash be classed as a disaster? Why? Why not?
- What is the Richter scale?

Comprehension

Check students' understanding of disasters with questions such as these:

- What sort of damage do some of the disasters we have already discussed cause?
  - to property
  - to people
- Have you ever experienced a disaster or even a minor disaster?
- What was it like? How did you feel during this experience?

Application

- Organize a visit to your nearest science center to provide students with an insight into earthquake movement.
- Pose this question: Can you predict or imagine what this classroom might look like if we were involved in an earthquake or a cyclone?
- Ask: What would the school and playground be like if they had been in the path of a wildfire?
- Have the students find out about the San Andreas fault. Ask them where it is and why it is so well-known.

Analysis

- Have students brainstorm the difference between a natural and a people-made disaster.
- Ask students to name recent disasters which fit into these categories.
- Ask: Which type of disasters do you think would be more frightening? Why?
- Have students work in small groups to investigate whether they can find any patterns emerging in the places where natural disasters have occurred.
- Ask students to research the theory of plate techtonics.

Synthesis

- Have students work in groups to suggest ways in which the number and severity of people-made disasters could be reduced.
- Have students brainstorm all organizations whose main functions are to develop ways to avoid disasters or at least reduce their effects on communities.
- Ask: Which country leads the world in forecasting the occurrence of earthquakes? Why do you think this is so?

Evaluation

- Ask: How and when is a tragic event classified as a disaster?
- Have students work in small groups to brainstorm ways in which they could minimize the outcomes of some of these disasters.
- Ask: What are some occupations in which it is crucial to have up-to-date knowledge of weather forecasts? Why?

Questioning and Brainstorming Skills for Social Studies

Knowledge, Application, Analysis

◗ ■ ✖ ★

Map Work

On a map of the world, name and indicate the position of

- active volcanoes

- recent earthquake zones

- tornado or cyclone areas

◗ ■ ✖ ★

Models

Work in a group of 3 or 4. Choose one of the following disasters for a five-minute oral presentation to the class.

- Earthquakes

- Cyclones

- Volcanic Eruptions

- Landslides/Avalanches

You can use photographs, diagrams, or models.

◗ ■ ✖ ★

National Weather Service

Find out from the National Weather Service how their work helps to minimize the affects of:

- hurricanes
- heat waves
- tornadoes
- flooding

◗ ■ ✖ ★

Plagues and Pests

In pairs, brainstorm the following:

- What was the Black Plague?

- What diseases are caused by mosquitos?

- What damage is done by locusts?

Then research to see if you were correct.

Name:

Disasters Around the World

Analysis,
Synthesis, Evaluation

TASK 1: Many natural disasters are made worse
by human activity.

Give an example for each one of these:

Disaster	Human Activty
Floods	
Forest fires	
Landslides	
Famines	
Earthquakes	

TASK 2: Illustrate two recent man-made disasters.

Brainstorm ways the disaster could have been avoided or the
damage reduced.

1:	2:

Ways to Avoid Disaster 1	Ways to Avoid Disaster 2

Make Your Own Task Cards

Renzulli's Enrichment Triad

Notes and Activities

by Fay Holbert

Overview for the
Classroom Teacher

Introduction to Renzulli's Enrichment Triad Model

The Enrichment Triad Model was devised by Joseph Renzulli in 1983 as a framework to provide students with the skills to carry out their own research investigations. Renzulli believes that all students should be given the opportunity to develop higher order thinking skills and pursue enriched high-end learning.

When implementing the Enrichment Triad Model in the classroom, the teacher's priority is the development of independence and encouragement of self-directed learning. The open-endedness of this model gives students the freedom to make choices about topics, resources, and manner of presentation. Teachers will also find a freedom in structure that allows them to guide their students through investigations and projects step by step, while still being able to change the process to suit the needs of individual students.

The Three Types of Activities

There are three types of activities within the Triad Model. They are the following:

Type I — exploratory experiences. Students' interests are identified. Students are given the opportunity to explore something new and extend their learning within a familiar topic.

Type II — group training activities. These activities promote the development of thinking and feeling processes with a major focus on advanced levels of thinking. These activities provide students with the necessary skills to carry out individual and small group investigations and include the following:

- creative and critical thinking skills
- decision making
- problem solving
- communication skills
- research skills

These activities develop "learning how to learn" skills. They focus on:

- becoming more creative
- research techniques
- how to use different types of equipment

Type III — individual and/or small group investigations of real issues. Students use appropriate methods of research and inquiry and develop management plans to aid in completion of the investigation.

Type I and II enrichment activities provide the basic skills needed for students to carry out their own or group investigations. Type III enrichment activities require a high level of commitment from the students and actively engage them in the learning process by expecting them to add new knowledge, ideas, or products to a field of study. (**Note**: Ensure that students have participated in Type I and Type II activities before embarking on a Type III activity.)

All three types of enrichment activities are interrelated to a high degree within the model. The diagram below illustrates this interrelation.

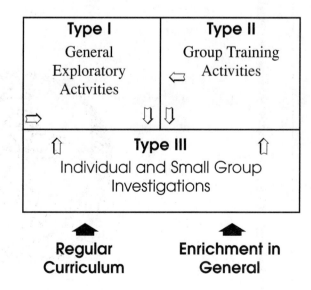

Overview for the
Classroom Teacher

Classroom Management

The Enrichment Triad Model emphasizes high quality outcomes for students that reflect the amount of understanding and the depth of thought of participating students. Depending upon ability in relation to the task at hand, students may start at any point within the model; however, allowing students to embark on Type III activities without background knowledge and training (Type I and II activities) may result in a poor or less than worthwhile investigation.

Type I

Students need to be given freedom to explore a variety of topics. This exploration must be purposeful and students must come up with some ideas for what they would like to study and how they will go about this.

For example, student may be interested in insects. The student then looks at material related to insects and develops questions to be investigated. These may include the following:

- Why do insects only have six legs?

- Do all insects have the same body structure?

- What does an insect do?

The student will also come up with a plan to find the information to answer these questions. For example the student might:

- interview the curator at a local museum

- find and observe insects in their natural habitat

Teachers need to help students identify areas of study and stimulate their interest. To start the process, ask students to talk about their interests. Once a student has identified an area of interest, the teacher needs to keep checking on progress by holding formal and informal meetings to discuss findings.

Type I activities should assist the teacher to decide which Type II activities need to be taught to particular groups of students.

Type II

As these activities are training exercises to help the student deal more effectively with finding content, the teacher must ensure that the skills are first taught in a content-free lesson. Once the skills are internalized, the student can apply them to a specific task.

These skills focus on critical analysis, problem solving, and divergent and creative thinking.

Type III

Not all students pursue an individual or small group investigation for every topic. Type III enrichment activities are designed to do the following:

- foster a desire to find out more about a topic of interest

- provide an opportunity for those students who have shown interest, willingness, and commitment to carry out an investigation of their own

- actively engage students in the formulation of a real issue and decision about a plan of action

- encourage students to produce new information for their topic and to present their findings to audiences for whom there is some relevance

Renzulli's Enrichment Triad for English

General

- Mastery of basic competencies in all areas needs to be made efficiently and rapidly through presentation that is exciting and relevant.

- Provide activities that are extra to the regular curriculum.

- Where necessary, provide opportunities for students to attend higher grades to participate in curriculum extension work.

- Arrange for students to work with mentors from within the school community or the local area.

- Take into account students' specific content interests and learning styles.

- Ensure that Type I activities involve little structure, but give some idea as to the type of investigation to be undertaken.

- Ensure that most enrichment activities are Type III activities.

Type I

- Set up interest centers related to themes or fields of study. These are to provoke curiosity rather than simply present information. Examples:
  - Writing: Include advertising, literary criticism, journalism, poetry, play writing, short stories, autobiography, etc.
  - Insects: Include fiction and non-fiction; start an ant farm; display dead insects.

- Invite authors to talk to the students about how they write their books.

- Conduct brainstorming activities where students list everything they wish to know about a topic.

- Organize field trips to observe and gather information, for example, to planetariums, museums, newspapers, or radio stations, etc.

Type II

- Develop research skills—present the research cycle and carry out basic research projects. Examples:
  - Why do bees perform a dance on returning to the hive?
  - What do authors include in biographies?

- Involve students in small-scale investigations requiring them to collect, record and communicate new information. For example, compare the different types of advertising seen on TV during children's shows and between 6:30 and 7:30 p.m.

- Develop problem-solving strategies for your students. Ask questions that require problem identification, analysis, and solution generation, at the same time developing an awareness of consequences of actions. Examples:
  - Imagine that telephone communications have been destroyed. How would we communicate quickly with other countries and areas?

Type III

- Ask students to formulate an issue and devise a plan of action to carry out the investigation.

- Provide ample time for individuals or small groups to carry out their investigations. Help them to develop a schedule and build in regular progress checks.

- Encourage students to produce new information. Examples:
  - Write a book.
  - Develop a new product and its advertising campaign.

Name:

Type I—Advertising

Form a small group. Choose a half-hour commercial TV program for each member to watch and note the advertisements. (If possible, tape the advertisements.) Select eight of these ads and complete the following questions:

1. Write down the products advertised.

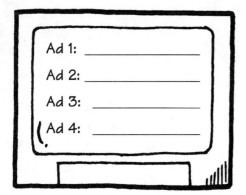
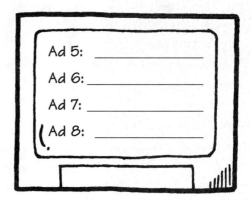

2. Which ad did you like best and why? _____

    _____

    _____

3. Choose two ads and write down what they said the product could do.

Product 1	Product 2
Name _____	Name _____

4. Identify the words used to persuade you to buy the product.

5. On a separate sheet:

    (a) Find an ad for one of these products in a magazine or newspaper. Compare it to the TV commercial.

    (b) Write down the steps you would take when conducting an advertising campaign for a new product.

Name: _____

Management
Strategies:

◗ ✚ ⊃ ❖

RENZULLI'S
TRIAD

English

BLM 38

Type III—Investigation Plan

General Area of Study: _____

Specific Area of Study: _____

What will I need to do to get started?		List everything needed to start, for example, information needed to know, surveys needed to conduct, etc.
What resources will I need?		List reference material for information, any people you may need to talk to or get help from.
How will I go about my investigation?		List ways you'll gather your information - interviews, surveys, observations.
Who is my intended audience?		List the different types of people or groups interested in your findings or product.
How am I going to share my information?		List how you'll present your information.

Self-Evaluation

Things I did well:	Things I could do better:
Resources that were useful:	**Things that did not give me the information I needed:**

Renzulli's Enrichment Traid for English

Theme: Egypt

→ ● ◗ ♣

Type I

Egyptology

In a group of three, brainstorm questions you would ask the following:

- the curator of a museum about Egyptian artifacts
- the Egyptian Consulate about Egypt

❖ ⇒ ✖

Type II

Pyramid Capers

Describe the different types of buildings the Egyptian Pharaohs built.

List the methods used by the Pharaohs to build these.

Make a model of one of the pyramids.

Label the model, including the Pharaoh who built it and why.

❖ ■ →

Type I

Investigating Egypt

From books on Egypt, pick a topic you would like to know more about.

Write down all the things you already know about your topic.

Write down at least six things you would like to find out about your topic.

⊃ ❖ ✶ ✖

Type II

Eco-Egypt

Many tourists visit the pyramids every year. The number of tourists walking on the pyramids and the erosion caused by the wind and the age of the structures are proving to be problems for the government of Egypt.

- Describe what the problems could be.

- Suggest how they could be overcome.

Renzulli's Enrichment Triad for English

Theme: Insects

Type I

Bugs at Play

Find some insects.

Write down where you found them.

Observe these insects over three days and write down what you see the insects doing.

Type II

Critter Cartography

With two friends, walk around the school grounds looking for areas where insects live.

Write down what these areas look like. (Find at least three different areas.)

Draw a map of the school and mark the location of your insect habitats.

Compare your map and details with other members of the class.

Type I

Bug Fan Club

From books on insects, choose a creature you think is interesting.

Write five questions you would ask a bug expert to gain more information about this insect.

List all the words you can think of that would describe this insect. Be as creative and thorough as you can.

Draw your insect and surround it with these words.

Type II

Antz

Watch the video *Antz*.

List some of the problems faced by the ant colony in this movie and the solutions they came up with.

With a friend, come up with some alternative solutions to these problems.

Create a flow chart of your various solutions, including the consequences of each.

Renzulli's Enrichment Triad for Math

General

- Ensure that students have a solid grasp of concepts through sequential developmental instruction in all areas of mathematics.

- Design contracts and guidelines with realistic completion dates.

- Create skill centers that help students apply and extend particular skills (addition, subtraction, multiplication, division, problem solving) in real-life situations.

- Provide games that involve logic. For example: triominoes, chess, and mastermind.

Type I

- Provide task cards that ask students to brainstorm ideas for solving mathematical problems. Example:
  - How many ways can you express the value shown by the numeral 5 in 756?

- Ask students to think of all the ways they use math in everyday life.

- Give students mathematical terms and examples of their application in real-life situations.

- Invite a builder, carpenter, interior designer, or architect to talk about the use of mathematics in his/her profession in relation to the following:
  - working out materials to be used and their cost
  - determining angles and pitches
  - drawing to scale and interpreting scale drawings

Type II

- Assist students to develop skills in making and checking predictions by providing mathematical problems requiring them to devise questions for given answers. Examples:
  - Answer: There were only 14 students left on the bus.
  - Answer: The travelers traveled 36 kms each day.

- Assist students to develop collecting, recording and communication skills by devising small group research projects.

- Enhance students' research and reporting skills. Example:
  - Provide students with the properties (size, color, shape, dimension, etc.) of less known objects. Ask them to name the objects and then sort them into different groups according to two like attributes (size and color; usefulness and/or popularity).

- Ask students to identify and analyze problems and come up with various solutions.

Type III

- Assist students to work out their own plans for completion of their chosen topics before beginning their research projects.

- Ask students to prepare and give a talk, predicting the outcome, prior to starting the project. On completion of the project, students give another talk to confirm or refute their original predictions.

- Hold a Math Fair where students present individual or small-group research projects to other grades.

Name:

Management
Strategies:

RENZULLI'S
TRIAD

Math

BLM 39

Type I—Everyday Math

Every day we use many different types of mathematical operations.

1. Look at the following activities and write down all the things you would do involving mathematics. We have done one for you. (Write your answers on the back of this sheet or on a separate sheet of paper.)

Buying three ice cream cones

1. Find the cost of one cone.
2. Multiply that cost by three.
3. Check that you have enough money to pay for the ice cream cones.
4. Check that you were given the correct change.

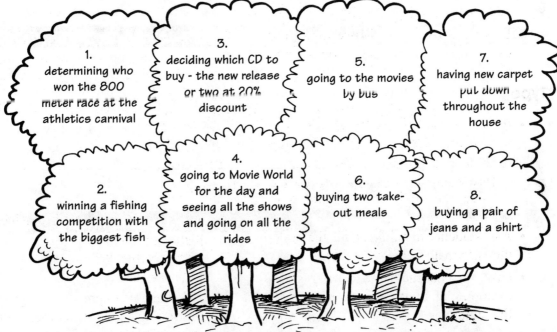

1. determining who won the 800 meter race at the athletics carnival

2. winning a fishing competition with the biggest fish

3. deciding which CD to buy - the new release or two at 20% discount

4. going to Movie World for the day and seeing all the shows and going on all the rides

5. going to the movies by bus

6. buying two take-out meals

7. having new carpet put down throughout the house

8. buying a pair of jeans and a shirt

2. With a friend, write down all the things you do during the day. Sort them into things that involve math and things that don't.

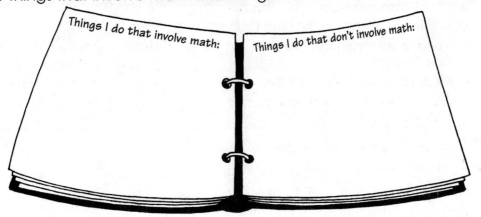

Things I do that involve math:

Things I do that don't involve math:

Name: _____

Type III—Investigating Math

Topic of my investigation: _____

Before I begin my investigation:

Things I may need to do	Things I may need to find out
Things I hope to find out	**What I hope to do with my findings**

After completing my investigation

Things I needed to do	What I had to know
What I found out	**What I will do with my findings**

Did your predictions match with what you really did and what you found out?

_____

_____

_____

Renzulli's Enrichment Triad for Math

Theme: Shopping

Type I

Sale Time

Collect flyers from different supermarkets.

Which supermarket is offering

- the cheapest breakfast cereal

- the cheapest sliced ham

- the most expensive margarine?

Discuss with a friend why different supermarkets have different items on sale. Note your ideas.

Type II

C(ash) D(istribution)s

New release CDs sold through music stores usually cost between $19.95 and $24.95. Part of the profit from each sale goes to the artist who recorded the CD.

With two or three friends, find out where the rest of the money goes.

Draw a diagram of this.

Type II

Supermarket Survey

In a small group, plan and write a survey to find out which local supermarket is the most popular for weekly shopping and why.

Survey students from other grades.

Present your findings pictorially —bar graphs, photographs, or pie graphs.

Make some statements about the shopping habits of your survey group.

Type II

Roll up ... Roll up

The class is to have a Math Fair.

Design an invitation to the Fair to be given to people you would like to attend.

Design a poster to advertise your presentation, stating why it is the best topic to be presented at the Fair.

Renzulli's Enrichment Traid for Math

Theme: Living Math

Type I ♣ → ■

Working Math

List as many different people as you can who use math every day in their professions.

Choose two of these.

Write down five questions to ask these people about how they use math in their professions.

Type II ❖ ▼ ❖

Tricky Terminology

What if the different types of angles (right angle, acute, obtuse) hadn't been discovered and named and we didn't use degrees to measure angles?

- How would we refer to the meeting places of lines?
- How would we measure how big these meeting places are?
- What other mathematical areas would be affected by the non-discovery of angles and degrees and their relationships?

Type II ✖ ⇒ ◆

Design with Numbers

With a friend, design a house floor plan. It must consist of 4 bedrooms, a kitchen, living room, bathroom, laundry room, dining room, family room, and garage.

- Work out the area of each room and the total area of the house.
- Work out how much it will cost to carpet and tile the inside of the house.
- Show where you would place this house on a rectangular block of land that measures 9,000 square feet (3,000 square meters).

112

Renzulli's Enrichment Triad for Science

General

- Create learning centers related to themes across curriculum areas or devoted to different areas of science: meteorology, ecology, pollution, astrology, genetics, electronics, biology, famous scientists, etc.

- Ensure that students have mastered terms and concepts related to science by exposing them to a curriculum that is developmental.

- Help students learn to solve problems creatively — there is not always a right or a wrong answer.

- Encourage students to question what they see: How did that happen?

- Encourage curiosity with displays showing an end result rather than the beginning only. Example:
  - different paper airplanes that fly well, and cards that ask for students' opinions as to why they fly so well.

Type I

- To arouse curiosity about how science works, provide simple experiments for students to perform.

- To create interest, display newspaper and magazine articles about different topics related to themes or science disciplines. Example:
  - inventions related to air travel
  - life cycles of living things such as toads and frogs, butterflies, cicadas, etc.

- Organize a trip to a local science center.

- Invite guest speakers to talk about their areas of interest.

Type II

- Encourage the development of divergent questioning skills by using open-ended questions. Examples:
  - List the ways in which birds find food.
  - Compare a moth's life cycle to that of a human being.

- Ask students to collect, record, and communicate their findings when solving crime scenes using different forensic science techniques.

- Organize students for a walk around the playground/local area (supervised) to observe and write down the different animals, birds, and insects, noting the number and location of the creatures. Students can then present these observations to the class either orally, in writing, or as diagrams.

- Ask students to complete research topics to help them identify methods, questioning techniques, and information gathering strategies.

Type III

- Ask students to identify why they wish to follow through with their investigations and why they are being done individually or in a small group.

- Ask students to identify their audience and present their findings appropriately.

- Engage mentors, peer tutors, parents, and other teachers to help students carry out and complete their investigations.

Name:

Management
Strategies:

Type I—Inventions

1. From books on inventions, choose one that you would like to investigate.

    The invention I will investigate is_____

2. Write down five things that you already know about this invention.

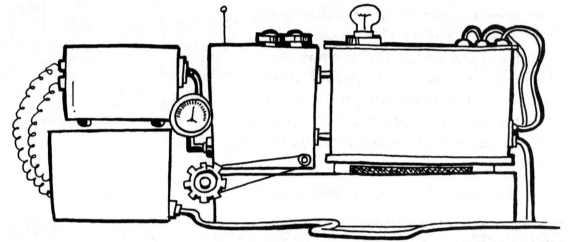

3. Write down four things that you would like to know about this invention.

    1. _____   3. _____

    2. _____   4. _____

4. Change one component in this invention. What effect would this have?

    The component I changed: What the new component looks like:

    _____   _____

    _____   _____

    _____   _____

    How it will work now: Did I improve the invention?

    _____   _____

    _____   _____

    _____   _____

Name:

Management
Strategies:

RENZULLI'S
TRIAD

Science

BLM 42

Type II—Forensic Science

With your forensic science team—photographer, fingerprint expert, questioner (decides who to question and what to ask), microscope analyst (decides what to take as evidence)—describe the steps you would take to solve the following crime:

The library office has been ransacked after the annual Book Fair and it looks like there has been a struggle. There is a note saying, "Thank you for the holiday money. It is greatly appreciated." The librarian and a large sum of money are missing. Three staff members (the assistant principal, the PE teacher, and the math teacher) were seen leaving the school grounds late on the day of the crime.

1.   Write down what each expert would do in the order they would do it

Photographer	Fingerprint Expert
1 _____	1 _____
2 _____	2 _____
3 _____	3 _____
4 _____	4 _____
Questioner	**Microscope Analyst**
1 _____	1 _____
2 _____	2 _____
3 _____	3 _____
4 _____	4 _____

(Use a separate sheet of paper.)

2.   How does your team think the crime took place?

3.   How will your team prove your suspicions?

4.   Write down how you will present your findings to the court so that your suspect will be convicted of this crime.

Renzulli's Enrichment Triad for Social Studies

General

- This area of the curriculum should be linked with as many other areas as possible.
- Within Social Studies, areas that can be explored include anthropology, demography, philosophy, genealogy, consumerism, etc.
- Create learning centers that explore universal themes and values such as family, friendship, conformity, initiative and vision, peace and independence, etc.
- Assist students to identify different aspects of communication: point of view, evaluative judgements, arguments, subjectivity and objectivity, empathy, prejudice, etc.

Type I

- Ask students to identify areas they would like to study. Group students according to their interests and ask them to identify particular areas to investigate.
- Organize a brainstorm about issues to do with the community, present government, and school rules. Group these into broad areas and develop a web of related issues that students may wish to pursue.
- Present videos about how communities get along. Ask students to identify issues and solutions portrayed in the video.
- Provide students with task cards from identified areas of interest.
- Visit the local council, State, or Federal governments to observe how decisions are made and how these forums are conducted.

Type II

- Engage students in discussions that involve moral and ethical issues.
- Ask students to prepare and complete questionnaires, surveys and interviews that require them to search for and state their values, attitudes and beliefs on topics. For example:
  - People with blue eyes are superior to people with green or brown eyes.
  - People who have a disability are not as clever as those who do not have a disability.
- Organize student role plays related to government decision making. Students take on roles of specific members of government and debate a topic from that member's point of view.
- Ask students to find out the demography of the local community and identify the different groups represented. Identify the needs of the community and write letters to local government bodies in relation to these.

Type III

- Involve students in an individual or small group investigation of their own choosing.
- Assist students in planning their investigation. Have them list how they intend to conduct it and the help they may need along the way.
- Ask students to present the findings of their investigation to the rest of the class or to other interested parties. Encourage them to use a variety of media and presentation forms.

Name:

Management
Strategies:

RENZULLI'S
TRIAD

Social Studies

BLM 43

Type I, II—Local Government

Plan to visit a public meeting of your local government.
Answer the following questions before the visit.

What do you expect to see at the meeting?	
What do you think the members will be discussing?	
What do you think the job of the mayor or manager involves?	
Write three questions you would like to ask during question time:	

Answer the following questions after the visit.

Who was at the meeting?	
What was discussed?	
What does the mayor or manager do?	
Were you satisfied with the answer to your questions?	

Having visited the meeting, what
aspect of local government would you
like to investigate?

_____

_____

_____

Renzulli's Enrichment Triad for Creative Arts

General

- Students should be able to experience all aspects of this curriculum during free time as well as during specific learning experiences.
- Ensure that students experience all aspects of creative thinking such as fluency, flexibility, originality, elaboration, curiosity, complexity, risk-taking and imagination.
- Include in this area of study: periods of art; contemporary artists; art and its contribution to society; design related to clothes, toys, furniture, buildings; calligraphy; animated film making; graphics; and puppetry.
- Display around the room art works by great masters, students, and local artists.

Type I

- Invite local artists to talk about how they produce their work.
- Arrange for local artists to conduct workshops in a variety of media.
- Visit an art gallery or view slides of works by masters and discuss these in different terms. For example: like/dislike; texture; form; color; tone; and line.
- Provide different media for students to work with and allow them to experiment with techniques.

Type II

- Organize debates about the techniques of twentieth century artists such as Andy Warhol.
- Ask students to research the life and work of an artist. On completion, group students according to the style of the various artists chosen. Ask them to discuss similarities or differences in their works.
- Show students pictures of different styles of houses (Federation, modern, Elizabethan, etc.) and ask them to discuss the design features of each.
- Discuss with students how art has reflected society over the ages.
- Ask students to design an item of clothing that could have been worn during Elizabethan times or during the 1960s.
- Ask students to critique their own art works for a school magazine.

Type III

- Students produce a piece of artwork using a technique of their own.
- Assist students in producing a plan of their artwork including initial sketches and preliminary thoughts on how the piece will look.
- Assist students in planning a time line for the completion of their artwork.
- Hold an exhibition of student artwork for the school and local community.

Name:

Type II—Puppetry

Design three puppets which demonstrate the effects of habitat destruction. They must not be made from anything that would lead to habitat destruction.

1. In the spaces below, jot down your first ideas for the three puppets.

Puppet 1	Puppet 2	Puppet 3

2. On a separate sheet of paper, plan what your puppet will look like and how you will make it.

3. Explain each puppet's connection to habitat destruction and how it will help get the message about the effects of this across to others.

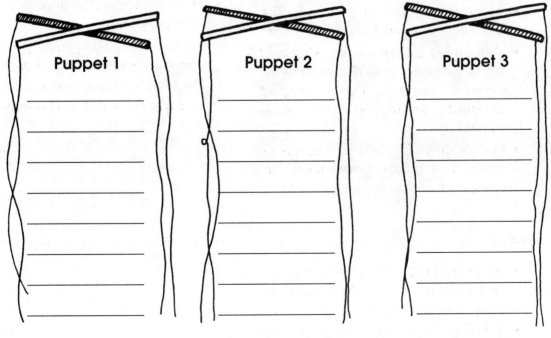

Thinking Caps
Notes and Activities

by Fay Holbert

Overview for the
Classroom Teacher

THINKING
CAPS

NOTES

Introduction to Thinking Caps

The thinking caps are inspired by Dr. de Bono's concepts in teaching thinking skills. They provide a means whereby students can identify and utilize all their thinking processes when faced with an issue. They also help students to discuss their thinking processes.

Each cap represents a different thinking approach:

Cap	Uses	Purpose	Questions to ask
Feelings Cap	• Making feelings known • Assessments and choices	• Alternatives • Emotions, feelings • Hunches, intuition	Which one do I like best? How do I feel about this?
Positive Cap	• Good points • Benefits • Why it will work • Likelihood	• Assessing and valuing • Extracting benefits • Making something work	Why is this worth doing? How will it help us? Why can it be done? Why will it help us?
Negative Cap	• Check for evidence • Check for logic • Feasibility • Impact • Weaknesses	• Find weaknesses • Makes assessments	Is this true? Will it work? What are the weaknesses? What is wrong with it?
Creative Cap	• Generate reactive ideas • Start ideas • Further, better, new ideas	• Creativity • Gives possibilities and alternatives	What are some ways to work this out /solve the problem? What ideas do we have?
Research Cap	• Identify what is relevant /most important/valid • Identify the information we have/need • Identify how to get the information we need	• Stimulate thinking • Check thinking	What information do we have? What information do we need to get?
Planning Cap	• Define focus/purpose • Set out thinking plan or agenda • Make observations and comments • Decide on the next step • Define outcomes • Summarize	• Be constructive • Thinking about thinking	What have we done so far? What do we do next? What is the next step? (often whole group)

* These characters appear on the BLMs and task cards following to indicate some thinking strategies.

Overview for the Classroom Teacher

How Do the Caps Work?

The different caps allow students to approach an issue from six different points of view. Instead of trying to do everything at once, students learn to handle the different aspects of thinking one at a time. Finally, different aspects come together to give wide range thinking.

Our egos are very involved in our thinking. We get attached to an argument or an idea and find it difficult to stand back and be objective. The role playing in the thinking caps helps students to detach the ego from the thinking–"This is not me, but my positive cap speaking." With the thinking caps, if we don't like a suggestion, we know that there will always be a chance to criticize it with the negative cap and to express feelings with the feelings cap. Meanwhile, it is possible to explore the idea with the research, positive and creative caps.

It is very important that every thinker is able to switch roles: put caps on and take caps off. The purpose and value of the thinking caps is to get students to use all six modes of thinking.

Beware: We tend to overuse the negative cap. We tend to under use the creative cap. When using the planning cap, be careful not to interrupt the line of thinking.

Four Styles for the Teacher to Use:

1. Put the cap on.

A child or a whole group:

"Give me some negative cap thinking."

"We're stuck. Can you put on your creative cap?"

2. Take the cap off.

Move away from a particular line of thinking:

"That's feeling cap thinking. Can you take off your feeling cap?"

"You've thought of lots of new ideas, but I think we should take off our creative caps now."

3. Switch caps.

This way we can call for a switch in thinking without hurting the student's feelings. We are not attacking the thinking, but asking for a change:

"We've heard the good things. Let's switch from the positive cap to the negative cap. What problems might there be if we do it like that?"

4. Signal your thinking.

Use the caps yourself and point out that you are using them as you teach the class.

Thinking Cap Sequences

The thinking caps are repeatedly used in sequence when we are confronted by more complicated thinking tasks. After a practice session, invite your students to recall the sequences they used. These observations provide a good basis for further discussions about the ways we approach thinking about problems and finding resolutions. Some common sequences are:

First Ideas: Planning – Research – Creative

Quick Assessment: Positive – Planning

Evaluation: Positive – Negative

Improvement: Negative – Creative

Explanation: Research – Creative

Direct Action: Feelings – Negative

Emotions: Feelings – Research – Creative – Planning

Caution: Research – Negative

Opportunity: Research – Positive

Design: Planning – Creative – Feelings

Possibilities: Creative – Planning

Useable Alternatives: Creative – Positive – Negative

Choice: Positive – Negative – Feelings

Final Assessment: Negative – Feelings

Thinking Caps for English

Theme: Clothing

Following are some thinking strategies on the theme of Clothing. Ask students to approach each question wearing the nominated caps. For example, when brainstorming "What is meant by clothing?," ask students to put on their planning caps first and define the focus of the question. Then ask them to change to their research cap and within the focus of the question, think of what they know clothing to be. Finally, ask them to put on their feelings caps so they can express their feelings about clothing.

First Ideas

- Brainstorm:
  - What is meant by 'clothing'? (Planning, Research, Feelings)
  - Why do we wear clothing? (All Caps)

Expansion and Explanation

- Ask students to consider clothing in different cultures with such questions as:
  - Are there any people who do not wear clothing? Why don't they? (Research, Creative, Feelings)
  - Why do people from different countries/areas wear different types of clothes? (Research, Creative, Feelings)
- Ask students to identify articles of clothing only worn by particular groups or nationalities.
  - Why do these groups/nationalities wear particular articles of clothing that other people do not wear? (Planning, Research, Feelings)

- Ask students to think about the concept of a 'national costume'.
  - Do you have a national costume?
  - Which national costumes are often seen in the media?
  - How are national costumes different from your everyday wear? (All Caps)

Changing Direction

- Brainstorm occupations found in the clothing industry. (Research, Creative)
- Why are clothes made from many different types of materials? (Planning, Creative, Research)
- Ask students about their own clothing.
  - Are you able to make, or help to make, any articles of clothing for yourself, or a member of your family?
  - What items are they?
  - How do you make them? (Planning, Research)

Wider Range Thinking

- Ask students to name some of the different clothes worn for different purposes.
  - Why do we have these different clothes? (Creative, Feelings, Research)
  - Why do different aged people wear different types/styles of clothing? (Creative, Planning, Feelings)

Name:

Clothing

1. List six things that affect the type of clothing people wear and make a note of how each thing makes a difference to their choices.

Influence	How does it make a difference?
1.	
2.	
3.	
4.	
5.	
6.	

2. In a small group quickly select 5 letters from the alphabet (do not include Q). Find an article of clothing beginning with each of these letters. In the table below, note what type of clothing it is, where it comes from, and who wears it.

Name of Item	What is it?	Where from?	Who wears it?
1.			
2.			
3.			
4.			
5.			

3. Now illustrate and label one of these articles of clothing.

Thinking Caps for English

▼ → ● ❖ ✚
Uniforms

What are uniforms?

Name six groups of people who wear uniforms.

Why do these people wear uniforms?

Find a colored picture of each of these people in uniform and create a mural for the classroom.

(Use all caps.)

→ ❖ ■ ◗ ⊃
Protective Clothing

Illustrate and label ten articles of clothing worn as protection in a work situation.

Which occupations need these clothes?

(Use positive, negative and research caps.)

▼ → ● ✶
What's in a Name?

How did these articles of clothing get their names?

Search through magazines to find pictures of them and label them with your answers.

Cardigan, Wellington boots,

Macintosh, Jodhpurs, Jeans,

Plus-fours, Cloche,

Driza-bone, Uniform,

Tee-shirt.

⊃ ✚ ⇒
Fashion Victim

Do you follow trends in the clothes you buy?

Why?

Name some clothing labels you like to wear?

Draw the trademark symbol of some of the brands you like best.

Name:

Clothing

1. Talking of items of clothing, what do these expressions mean?

Keep your shirt on. _____

Pull your socks up. _____

Treat her with kid gloves. _____

If the show fits, wear it. _____

He'd give you the shirt off his back. _____

2. How does climate affect the clothing you wear? Draw yourself sensibly dressed for the following conditions. Include any accessories you may also need.

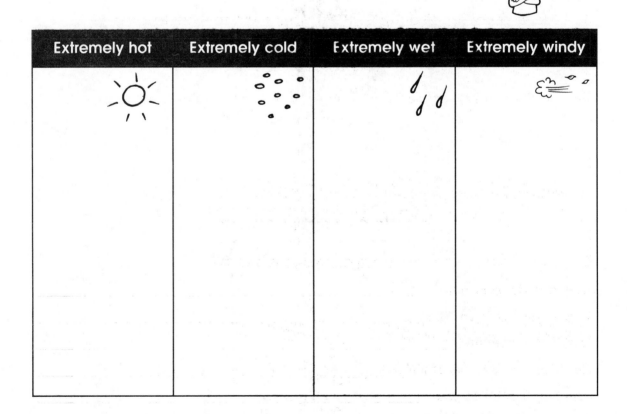

Extremely hot	Extremely cold	Extremely wet	Extremely windy

Management
Strategies:

▼ ❖ ■
★ ✳ ⇒

THINKING
CAPS

English

BLM 47

Hats

1. List, draw, and label as many types of hats as you can.
    Show:

    • who wears the hat

    • where you'll find them (in which country)

2. Why are there so many different types of head
    coverings?

    Give as many reasons as you can.

There are so many hats because: _____

_____

_____

_____

_____

3. Make a hat for all occasions. Put your mind to work to
    create a useful hat that is also formal, sporty,
    protective etc.

4. About hats, what do these expressions mean?

Keep it under your hat. _____

Throw your hat in the ring. _____

Pass the hat around. _____

He pulled a rabbit out of the hat. _____

I take my hat off to you. _____

Thinking Caps for Math

Theme: Math Can Be Fun

Following are some thinking strategies on the theme of Math Can Be Fun. Use the same approach as outlined at the beginning of the Thinking Cap for English section.

Quick Assessment/Getting Started

- Ask students to identify:
  - How many operations they can do in mathematics (Research)
  - Which mathematical instruments they use at school (Research)
- Ask students to collect these instruments to make a display and explain what each is used for. (Research, Planning)
- Brainstorm:
  - What do you like about math?
  - Why? (Feelings, Positive, Research)
  - What do you dislike about mathematics?
  - Why? (Feelings, Negative, Research)

Assessing and Valuing

- Ask students to consider:
  - Why mathematics is a compulsory subject? (Planning, Research, Creative)
  - If they did not know how to do any mathematics at all, what jobs would be available to them when they left school. (Planning, Positive, Negative, Research)
  - The consequences of relying on a calculator to solve all mathematical problems. (Negative, Creative, Planning, Feelings)
- Ask students what system of weights and measures we used before the decimal system. Ask them to:
  - Name as many of these measurements as they can.
  - Name any countries that still use this system. (Planning, Research)
- Brainstorm:
  - Why is our present decimal system of weights and measures easier to use than the previous system? (Research, Positive)

Research

- Find out about different mathematicians. (Research, Positive)
- Look at different mathematical systems. (Research)
- Identify mathematical terms and other words relating to numbers. (Research)
- Look at different currencies.

Stimulate Thinking and Creativity

- Ask students to list any short cuts (quick ways) they know to complete any operations in mathematics. For example, to multiply or divide by 10.
  - Explain any short cuts you know. (Research, Creative, Positive)

Name: _____

Management
Strategies:

THINKING
CAPS

Math

BLM 48

Math Facts

1. Use your research skills to find information about what these Greek mathematicians did to help students of mathematics:

Thales   Pythagoras

Euclid   Archimedes   Eratosthenes

2. Complete this table to show the numerals from 1 to 10 (more if you can) in the Greek, Roman, Mayan, and Arabic systems:

Hindu-Arabic (ours)	Greek	Roman	Mayan	Arabic
1				
2				
3				
4				
5				
6				
7				
8				
9				
10				

3. What numbers do these words relate to?

pair	_____	quire	_____	gross	_____
dozen	_____	century	_____	octave	_____
decimal	_____	score	_____	uniform	_____
binary	_____	quadrangle	_____	millennium	_____

Thinking Caps for Math

What's in a Number?

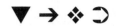

The name of each of the following things includes a reference to a number associated with the thing. Draw or make a model of each and provide labels.

Write a short description to go with each one.

tripod, unicorn, octopus, hexapod, pentagram, tricorn,

quintuplets, binoculars, centipede, dodecahedron.

Calculating

Draw a mathematical calculator like the one you use at school.

Write and practice a short talk explaining how to use the calculator to a younger student at your school.

Brilliant Beads and String

Draw an abacus.

Which people first used the abacus?

Create a short demonstration explaining to someone who has never seen an abacus how it is used and who uses it.

Money and Math

Management Strategies:

THINKING CAPS

Math

BLM 49

1. In which countries are these money units used? From the newspaper, find the value of our dollar against these currencies. Does this exchange rate stay constant? Why/why not?

Currency	Country	Exchange Rate with Dollar
Rupee		
Lira		
Baht		
Yuan		
Zloty		
Escudo		
Krona		
Rand		
Rouble		

2. What is the correct name for the things described below?

Description	Name	Description	Name
500 sheets of paper		200th anniversary	
Dinosaur with three horns on its head		Married to two people at the same time	
Four babies at the same time born to one mother		Roman officer in charge of 100 soldiers	
Six-pointed star		10-event athletic competition	
Three-sided figure		5-event athletic competition	

Name:

Puzzles

1. Consecutive numbers are those which follow each other in counting order, for example: 2, 3, 4.

Many numbers can be made by adding consecutive numbers, for example:

9 = 4 + 5 and 10 = 1 + 2 + 3 + 4

On a clean sheet of paper, list down the page numbers from 1 to 30. Beside each, show the consecutive numbers which add up to make that original number. (Do not use zero.)

Using different colored highlighters, show which numbers use 2, 3, or more consecutive numbers.

Are there any you can't do?

What do you notice about the numbers made by adding 3 consecutives?

2. The missing numbers in this puzzle are the digits 1 to 9. Each digit is used only once. Complete the puzzle, using the clues below.

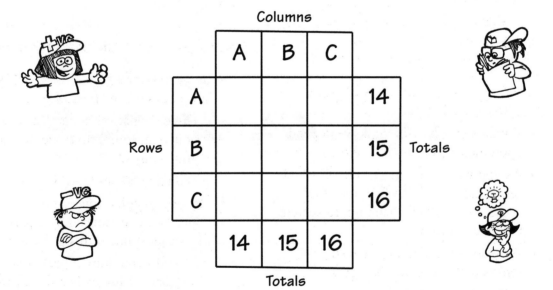

Columns

	A	B	C	Totals
A				14
B				15
C				16
Totals	14	15	16	

Rows

Clues:

✎ Row A has all even digits.   ✎ Row B has all odd digits.

✎ 4 and 6 are in the same column.   ✎ 6 is not in the same row as 4.

✎ 1 and 9 are in the same row.

Thinking Caps for Health

Theme: Our Senses

Following are some thinking strategies on the theme of "Our Senses." Use the same approach as outlined at the beginning of Thinking Caps for English.

Getting Started/Quick Assessment

- Name the five senses. (Research)
- Which organs of your body are responsible for the work done by your five senses? (Research)
- Which organ is the "master controller" of your five senses? (Research)

More Assessment and Valuing

- How do your senses help you to learn? Discuss each one:
  - sight
  - hearing
  - smell
  - taste
  - touch (All Caps)
- Which sense do you think we depend upon most? (Research, Feelings)
- As you walk home from school, which senses do you use? What does each sense do for you? (Planning, Research, Positive, Negative)
- Why do some animals have some senses that are better than ours?
  - Which animals?
  - Which senses? (Research, Feelings, Creative, Planning)

Explanation and Valuing

- Ask students to consider:
  - Why do some people love the taste of a particular food, while other people don't like it at all? (Positive, Negative, Feelings)
  - Why does a bump on the nose hurt more than an equal bump on your arm or leg? Why does a minute particle of grit cause real pain when it is in your eye, but doesn't bother you if it is in your hair? (Research, Feelings, Planning)
  - How can constant, or sudden very loud noise cause deafness, or partial deafness? Give examples of such noises. (Planning, Research, Negative)

Speculation and Creative Thinking

- Can you improve your senses? If so, how could this be possible?
  - Under what circumstances would you want to improve one or more of your senses?
  - Which one/ones? (All Caps)
- Can you imagine some of the difficulties experienced by a person who has lost one of his or her senses?
  - How do you think a person who has lost one of his or her senses makes up for this?
  - Discuss each sense. (All Caps)

Thinking Caps for Health

❖ ■ ✖ ⊃

Seeing is Believing!

What are some things that you have learned by using:

  your sense of sight?

 your sense of hearing?

Plan a demonstration that shows how important one of these senses is to your survival and growth.

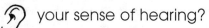

▼ ❖ ✚

Mouth Watering!

Ponder this question and come up with as many answers as you can think of:

How can your sense of taste help you, other than telling you that you like or dislike your food?

Create a poster telling your class about the sense of taste and what it does.

❖ ✖ ⊃ ⇒

Scratch and Smell

List all the ways you could be protected by your sense of smell.

Now list all the ways you could be protected by your sense of touch.

Write a brief report about the importance of these two senses to the survival of human beings.

→ ■ ⊃

Smelly Problems

If we want to get rid of a smell from the room, for example, a cooking smell, what can we do?

Choose four offensive smells and think of four ways to get rid of each. Write a brief explanation of why your methods will work.

(Use planning, creative, positive and negative caps.)

Name:

Management Strategies:

THINKING
CAPS

PDHPE

BLM 51

Our Senses

1. In pairs, try not using your sense of sight or your sense of hearing for a few minutes of normal classroom activities.

   • Ask your partner to blindfold you, so you really cannot see.

   • Use earplugs so you really cannot hear.

   Note your responses below:

   ### How difficult was it?

Without Sight	
Without Sound	

   ### How did you feel?

Without Sight	
Without Sound	

   ### What did you want your friends to do for or with you?

Without Sight	
Without Sound	

2. List the kinds of things you could do to help a person who has impaired sight or hearing.

   _____

   _____

3. **Seeing Eye Dogs**

   • How important are Seeing Eye Dogs for vision impaired people?

   • Which breeds are chosen for this work? Why?

   • Visit your local veterinary hospital or SPCA center and find out more information about the training and work done by these animals.

   • Report back to your class with your information.

Thinking Caps for Creative Arts

Theme: Natural Landscapes

First Thoughts/ Quick Assessment

- Ask students what they understand to be a landscape painting. (Research, Positive, Negative, Feelings)
- Display prints/photographs of some of landscape artists. Ask students questions such as:
  - Do you think they are realistic?
  - Why?/Why not? (Feelings, Research, Positive, Negative)

Research and Explore

- Visit an art gallery or photographic studio.
  - Compare and contrast work on display.
  - Speak with the curator or any artists who may be present, and question them about the work on display. (All Caps)
- Organize a visit to your local high school to speak with art students about their major works. Let students ask the older students such questions as:
  - Why have they chosen Art as one of their subjects?
  - What do they like about the subject?
  - What have they found difficult and how have they overcome these difficulties? (Creative, Planning, Research, Positive)
- Ask students to mix colors to get shades that duplicate the color of a given item. For example, a leaf, a flower, a piece of cloth, etc. (Planning, Creative, Research)
- Ask students to consider how important plants are in our lives. (All Caps)

Extrapolate

- Invite a local landscape gardener to your class to talk about his or her work, and what it entails. Identify areas where landscape gardeners have been employed. (All Caps)
- Ask students to consider such questions as:
  - How can our own landscape be changed by people? (Creative, Positive, Negative, Feelings)
  - How can our own landscape be changed by nature? (Creative, Positive, Negative, Feelings)
  - Can we do anything about this? (All Caps)

Wide Range Thinking/Creativity

- Ask students to consider how cave paintings or petroglyphs were done. (All Caps)
- Brainstorm:
  - What can we use to make our own paints in all of the colors that are needed? (All Caps)
  - How could we make our own brushes? (All Caps)

Thinking Caps for Creative Arts

Favorite Artists

Find one or two partners.

Choose an artist whose work you (all) like and research this artist in the library or use other research tools.

Present your group's findings to the class.

When all groups have reported back, discuss reasons for differences in the styles of the different artists presented.

Make Your Mark

Examine some cave paintings and discover the colors that have been used.

Make your own colors – dark brown, light brown— without using traditional paint.

Find paintings of an animal by a cave artist and, using the paints you have prepared, copy it to the best of your ability.

Model Landscape

Every year somewhere in the world there are fires, floods, storms—perhaps even an earthquake. Make a model of a ravaged area. Add your own ideas for the aftermath of this disaster, depicting the damage done.

Present your model to the class discussing:
- If anything has been done to lessen/avoid the devastation.
- If anything good will come from this situation.

(Use all caps.)

Name:

Landscape Design

Choose one or two partners.

1. Identify an outside area at your school or at home that could be redesigned. _____

_____

2. Record accurate measurements. (We have started the table for you.)

Length	Width	Perimeter		

3. List the features you would like to change and the features you would like to add. Consider the existing environment, colors, and shapes.

Features to Change	Features to Add

4. On a large sheet of paper, prepare a landscape design for the area. Using your measurements, draw your design to scale.

Show colors, shapes, sizes of gardens, pathways, trees, boundaries, seats, and other objects.

Make Your Own Task Cards

Gardner's Multiple Intelligences Notes and Activities

by Fay Holbert

Overview for the Classroom Teacher

GARDNER'S MULTIPLE INTELLIGENCES NOTES

Introduction to Howard Gardner's Multiple Intelligences

Gardner defines intelligence as "he ability to solve problems, or to create products, that are valued within one or more cultural setting/s". He maintains that it should be possible to identify an individual's educational profile at an early age, and then draw upon this knowledge to enhance that person's educational opportunities and options. An educator should be able to channel individuals with unusual talents into special enrichment programs. To this end, he has developed a framework, building on the theory of multiple intelligences, that can be applied to any educational situation.

Because of Gardner's work, many educators believe that education is not merely a means to sort out a few children and make them leaders, but to develop the latent talents of the entire population in diverse ways.

If we are to understand our children's potential, we must take into consideration all of their abilities and not just those that can be tested with standardized instruments such as an I.Q. test. What is important in educational terms is not which intelligences we are strongest in, but our own particular blend of strengths and weaknesses.

The importance attached to the I.Q. however is not entirely inappropriate – the score does predict a person's ability to achieve in school subjects. Its limitation is that it predicts little of the successes in later life.

So, what of the wider range of performances that are valued in different parts of the world? For example, consider a 12 year old boy from the Caroline Islands who is selected by his elders to learn how to become a master sailor and undertake study of navigation, geography, and the stars and a 15 year old Iranian youth who has committed to heart the entire Koran, mastered the Arabic language, and will train to be a teacher and religious leader.

It is obvious that these two young people are displaying intelligent behavior, and it is probable that the present method of assessing intellect is not going to allow an accurate assessment of their potential. Only if we expand and rethink our views of what counts as human intellect will we be able to devise more appropriate ways of assessing it and more effective ways of educating it.

Gardner's Intelligences are:

- Verbal/Linguistic
- Logical/Mathematical
- Visual/Spatial
- Bodily/Kinesthetic
- Musical/Rhythmical
- Interpersonal
- Intrapersonal

Recently, Gardner has added a new intelligence: Nature/Environmental

Learning Centers

The classroom teacher should give equal time and attention to each intelligence every day. One way to achieve this is to maintain various learning centers in the classroom. For example:

- The Shakespeare Center (**Verbal/ Linguistic**)
- The Einstein Center (**Logical/ Mathematical**)
- The da Vinci Center (**Visual/Spatial**)
- The Edison Center (**Bodily/Kinesthetic**)
- The Fitzgerald Center (**Musical/Rhythmical**)
- The Chisholm Center (**Interpersonal**)
- The Keller Center (**Intrapersonal**)
- The Leakey Center (**Nature/ Environmental**)

A Note About This Section

This section looks at one theme from the perspective of the various intelligences.

Overview for the Classroom Teacher

Details and Description of Gardner's Multiple Intelligences

Verbal/Linguistic (V/L)

The student who enjoys words – reading, writing, storytelling, humor/jokes. He/she participates eagerly in debates, story/poetry writing, journal/diary keeping, and has a sensitivity to language.

- Writer, poet, novelist, journalist, psycho-linguist (L/M), signing

Logical/Mathematical (L/M)

The student who loves numbers, patterns, relationships, formulae. He/she shines at mathematics, reasoning, logic, problem solving, and deciphering codes and enjoys pattern games, calculation, number sequences, and outlining.

- Scientist, mathematician, engineer, technician

Visual/Spatial (V/S)

The student who loves drawing, building, designing, creating, visualizing colors, pictures, observing, patterns/designs. He/she enjoys creating models, mind mapping, pretending and has an active imagination.

- Artist, cartographer, navigator, decorator, chess player

Bodily/Kinesthetic (B/K)

The student who has to touch, move, handle objects. He/she enjoys dance, drama, role play, mime, sports games, physical gestures, martial arts and is great with body control, refining movement, expression through movement, inventing, interaction.

- Athlete, surgeon (L/M), dancer/choreographer (M/R)

Musical/Rhythmical (M/R)

The student who loves sounds, melody, rhythm, playing instruments, singing, vocal sounds/tones. He/she needs to be involved with music composition/creation, music performances and enjoys percussion, humming, environmental/instrumental sounds, tonal and rhythmic patterns.

- Musician, composer, sound engineer (L/M), music critic (V/L)

Interpersonal (Ier)

The student who likes interacting, talking, giving and receiving feedback, group projects, cooperative learning strategies, division of labor. He/she needs to be involved in collaborative tasks and person to person communication. This student is always intuitive to others' feelings and motives and is empathetic.

- Administrator, coach, mental health, physician (L/M), teacher (various)

Intrapersonal (Ira)

The student who wants to work alone, pursue personal interests, understands self, has introspective feelings and dreams. He/she displays silent reflective methods, higher order reasoning and metacognition techniques, emotional processing, focus/concentration skills, and complex guided imagery, 'centering' practices.

- Writer (V/L), inventor (L/M)

Nature/Environmental (N/E)

Recently, Gardner has included an eighth intelligence which he calls Nature/Environmental. Not a lot of information is yet available from Gardner on this intelligence, but it is summarized as one involving the recognition and classification of species in the environment, and how we can best preserve this environment for the greatest benefit to all.

- Veterinarian, zoologist, botanist, national park ranger, landscape gardener (V/L), florist

Note: the students illustrated here appear on the task cards and BLMs that follow to indicate the intelligence to which that activity is primarily targeted.

Gardner's Multiple Intelligences Activities

Theme: Ancient Civilizations—What They Gave Us

Many of the activities that follow are not exclusive to one intelligence, but may involve two or more. For example, those asking for illustrations involve Visual/Spatial and those requiring oral and/or written presentations involve Verbal/Linguistic.

Where questions could be answered with a yes or no response, probe for more information.

The activities that follow concentrate mainly on civilizations BC.

Verbal/Linguistic
- What is the meaning of *civilization*?
- What is the meaning of *ancient*?
- What is meant by *hunters and gatherers*? How and why did this type of existence change?
- How many words can you find in your dictionary that derive from the Latin *civis*?
- Prior to writing, how were stories, facts and history kept and passed on?

Logical/Mathematical
- The Great Pyramid has a base that would hold six football fields. How does the school playground compare?
- The Great Pyramid is 40 stories high —approximately 138 meters. How many times taller than your school is that?
- Why would these people keep a *tally*?
- Why was it important to know the length of a year and of daylight?
- How large were cities 2500 years ago? Were they bigger than your town/city?
- What did farmers do with crops or animals they couldn't use?
- How were workers and slaves paid?
- How did farmers water their crops?

Visual/Spatial
- How often does your family read maps? What is your most commonly used map?
- On a map of the world, where were Sumer, Egypt, Mesopotamia, Crete, Greece, China, Persia, the Indus Valley? Are they still known by these names?

- Why were so many temples and palaces built?
- What do wall and cave paintings tell us?

Bodily/Kinesthetic
- What types of building skills were needed in ancient civilizations?
- What types of handcrafts were valued?
- What would children have played with?
- How might the men have kept fit for war?

Musical/Rhythmical
- Why were music and dance so important?
- What sort of musical/rhythmical instruments might have been used?
- Other than dance, why might a steady rhythm or clear sound have been important?
- What could have been used for making instruments?

Interpersonal
- What types of occupations existed?
- Who made laws in these towns and cities?
- How were they different from our laws?
- How did people travel?
- Were there equal rights for men and women? How do we know?

Intrapersonal
- Which civilization would you like to have been a member of? Which one would you not like to join? Why?
- Which occupation would you have chosen?
- Which invention/creation/development was the most important for mankind?

Nature/Environmental
- Why were the farmers soil rich?
- What is irrigation?
- What types of crops were grown?
- Which animals were kept?
- Why did these people only eat meat at celebrations?
- How were plants and animals used, other than for food?

Activities for Ancient Civilizations

GARDNER'S MULTIPLE INTELLIGENCES TASK CARDS

Alphabets

Find the answers to these questions:

1. Which people introduced the alphabet? When did this happen?

2. Why do you think these people wanted an alphabet?

3. In what ways was the alphabet such an important advance for humanity?

Lots of Alphabets

Why do you think different alphabets gradually came into existence?

Find examples of two other alphabets and write a brief description of how they developed. Reference dictionaries and encyclopedias are a good place to start your research.

Ancient Civilization Project

Select one ancient civilization to study in depth.

Create a presentation, using a project book or other media, about this civilization. Include:

Where the civilization was found, when it developed and was at its height, who its leaders were, what kinds of technology were developed, information about its culture, major achievements, and reason/s for its rise and fall.

Activities for Ancient Civilizations

Weights and Measures

As trade was one of the main reasons for the success or failure of a civilization, weights and measures were vital to both sellers and buyers.

One such weight measure was a *grain balance*. Draw a diagram of this.

With a partner construct a working model of the balance so you can demonstrate to the class how it worked.

The Importance of Ports

Why was it important for ancient civilizations to be near a river and/or the sea?

On a map of the world show where these civilizations were found:

Sumer, Phoenicia, Egypt, Babylon, Mycenae, Crete, Persia.

Are they still known by the same names?

Note their location in relation to water.

Ancient Arts and Crafts

Search through reference books, encyclopedias, and magazines to find pictures or photographs of the jewelry worn by the people of these ancient communities. Also find illustrations of the pottery created.

Do one of these activities:

1. Using beads, modeling clay, and nylon thread (and the illustrations you have found), create some replica jewelry of these times.

2. Paint and decorate an earthenware pot in the style of an ancient artisan.

Name:

Comparative Sizes

1.   Compare the size and capacity of these buildings:

Structure	Area of Base	Spectator Capacity
The Colosseum		
Stadium of Olympia		
Latest Olympic Stadium		

2.   Compare the dimensions of these buildings:

Structure	Length	Width	Height
Great Pyramid			
White House			
Your Home			

3.   What are the main differences between the ancient and the modern buildings in terms of how they have been built?

Write your thoughts here:

Did you know that the base of the Great Pyramid, completed in 2528 BC, is a perfect square to within 15 mm? During a period of about 20 years, 200,000 slaves moved 2,500,000 stones for its construction.

Town Planning

About 2500 BC, the people of the Indus Valley had town planners who planned the houses in city blocks, separated by roads 30 feet (9 meters) wide. They even drew city maps!

1. Draw a map of your community showing where you live, play, and learn.

2. What is the population of your town/city/suburb?

    _____

3. Over 3500 years ago the population of Babylon was approximately 200,000. Name six cities and/or towns that have a population approximately the same as ancient Babylon.

    1 _____   2 _____

    3 _____   4 _____

    5 _____   6 _____

4. What is the population of your country, according to the last census?

    _____

Did you know that a census taken about 2000 years ago in China showed that the Han-ruled states had a population of 59,594,978?

Name:

Measuring Time

Early civilizations had instruments for measuring time, but they were not very reliable.

1. Explain how these instruments operated and illustrate each one.

Sundial	Candle Clock
Water Clock	Hour Glass

2. Now complete the table below:

Timepiece	Where?	When?	Disadvantages
Sundial			
Water Clock			
Candle Clock			
Hourglass			

Management
Strategies:

GARDNER'S
MULTIPLE
INTELLIGENCES
BLM 56

Ancient Irrigation Systems

The growing cities of Babylon, Çatalhöyük, Memphis, and Mohenjo-Daro now had tradesmen, artisans and officials who traded their services for the food they needed. As a result, the farmers had to increase their food production. To do this they needed larger farms and a way to water their crops. They began to irrigate their land. They used a shaduf and later a treadmill.

1. Illustrate these two devices.

Shaduf	Treadmill

2. How did each help to irrigate the land?

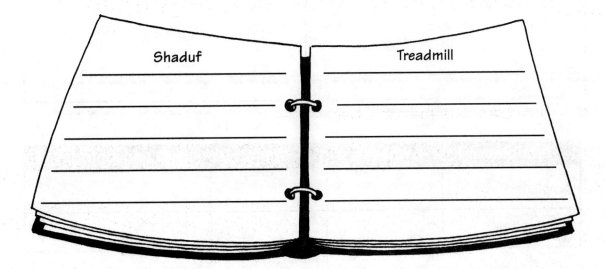

Shaduf   Treadmill

3. With a partner, make a model of a water wheel and demonstrate to the class how it functioned.

Activities for Ancient Civilizations

Ancient Musical Instruments

Using any materials, design and construct some basic musical instruments, like those played by the citizens of ancient cultures. Some ideas are:

- percussion – drum/tambourine
- stringed instrument – lute/viol
- woodwind – flute/recorder

Teach a group of your friends how to play your instruments. Compose a passage of rhythmical music to perform for your class or school assembly.

Original Toys

Toys were not very plentiful or varied for children thousands of years ago, but it is known that they had spinning tops and balls among their playthings.

Plan how you would make:

- A ball using grass, reeds, raffia, twine, etc.
- A spinning top

Make one or both of these toys. Now illustrate a pull-along toy that might have been made for a little child.

Ancient Services

The upper and middle class citizens of Rome and cities in the Indus Valley had central heating and a water supply (with sewerage) in their homes. They were also provided with a rubbish collection and disposal system for the city.

How do you think these facilities worked so many centuries ago?

Illustrate your thoughts.

Activities for Ancient Civilizations

GARDNER'S MULTIPLE INTELLIGENCES
TASK CARDS

The Importance of Music

Why were music and dance such important parts of the lives of the people who lived hundreds and thousands of years ago?

Complete this chart, giving some reasons:

Wealthy/Upper Class	Middle Class	Poorer Class/Slaves
1.		
2.		
3.		
4.		
5.		

Soldiers Health Regimen

Plan a daily health and physical fitness program for soldiers in the army of Sparta.

In some nations all men were required to be ready to go to war whenever their ruler decided to fight another nation.

Time	Food	Arms/Shoulders	Body	Legs

Activities for Ancient Civilizations

GARDNER'S MULTIPLE INTELLIGENCES
TASK CARDS

Olympic Games

In the Olympic Games, and other adult athletic competitions, what is the marathon?

Why is this event given this name?

Who won the very first Marathon?

The Importance of Coins

Business had been carried on using a trading or bartering system for many hundreds of years. Coinage was introduced in Persia about 500 BC and in China about 220 BC.

How would this have changed the daily activities of the traders and other business people?

Ancient Entertainment

How were the people entertained in Ancient Babylon,
Egypt, Athens, and/or Rome?

Illustrate some of their pastimes and amusements.

Government

Management
Strategies:

GARDNER'S
MULTIPLE
INTELLIGENCES

BLM 57

Over 2500 years ago the Greeks overthrew the aristocracy and installed a democracy.

1. What do these two words mean?

Aristocracy

Democracy

2. Illustrate how a democracy works:

In what ways was the Greek democracy different from ours?

_____

_____

_____

_____

_____

_____

_____

_____

_____

_____

3. Organize a democratic election for your class.

Name:

Ancient Medicine

Would you like to have been a doctor in Egypt or the Indus Valley, 2000 years ago?

The first known textbook on surgery was recorded by the Egyptians about 2500 BC.

The first hospital and rest homes were built in the Indus Valley by King Asoka about 300 BC.

If a doctor failed to heal a rich patient, he was severely punished, sometimes even killed. If he failed to heal a slave, his punishment was only a payment to the master.

1.   Who was Hippocrates and how do we remember him today?

   _____

2.   Who are some famous, more recent-day physicians and surgeons and what have they accomplished for society?

	Doctor	When?	What?
1.			
2.			
3.			
4.			
5.			
6.			
7.			

Activities for Ancient Civilizations

▼ → ❖ ✶ ✚

Jobs for the Boys

As boys grew up in ancient times they had a wide range of occupations to choose from—if they were not slaves.

Name some of the jobs that were open to boys in these areas:

• handcrafts

• sciences

• art

• building

• designing

→ ❖ ✶ ✚

Lives of Girls

As girls grew up, what did they plan for the future?

Make a list of all your ideas.

▼ ❖ ■ ✶ ⊃

Food: Then and Now

Research the types of food eaten in these ancient cultures.

What types of crops did farmers produce?

Make a list of all the kinds of food.

Now compare this to the food we eat today.

List those that are no longer eaten.

▼ → ● ❖ ✶ ⊃

Ancient Animals

Name the animals that were used for the purposes listed below:

1. as food

2. for work

3. in wars

4. as pets

5. in religious matters

Activities for Ancient Civilizations

Hammurabi's Codes

Hammurabi, King of Mesopotamia in about 1792 BC, brought great changes to the laws of his country. Two of his laws were:

1. Wrongdoers were judged and punished by the decision of the society, rather than by the victim and/or the victim's family.

2. All killings were treated as murder.

List the **advantages** and the **disadvantages** of these two laws.

Features of Ancient Civilizations

What can you find out about these features of ancient civilizations?

Quipu _____

_____

Ziggurat _____

_____

Petroglyphs _____

_____

Obsidian _____

_____

Shaduf _____

_____

Rosetta Stone _____

_____

The Wheel

Management
Strategies:

GARDNER'S
MULTIPLE
INTELLIGENCES
BLM 59

The wheel was first invented in Sumer about 3500 BC. By about 3250 BC the first wheeled vehicles were used there.

1. How do you think the idea of the wheel might first have come to the Sumerians? Write your thoughts here:

2. How might the first wheels have been made? _____

_____

3. List the improvements made by the wheel for these people.

Rulers	Traders	Farmers	Others

4. Which people might have benefited most from the wheel?

Illustrate your reasons here.

Make Your Own Task Cards

Notes

EXTENSION
ACTIVITY
BOOK

NOTES

Notes